BRONEMANN

LillIE

SMOOTH SAILING ALWAYS!

Once Upon a Tide

TALES FROM A FOXHOLE IN THE SOUTH PACIFIC

1982 OUT PRODUCTIONS 2000

BY LEROY B. BRONEMANN

ISBN 1-57921-281-6
Library of Congress Catalog Card Number: TX 331-137-1979

Dedication

"LeRoy, stop what you're doing—whatever it is, it can't be honest."

Minnie Bronemann (Mother), 1943

To my comrades of the 454th Amphibious Truck Company and those of the First Marine Division with whom we participated in the battles of Peleliu and Okinawa.

To my Army buddies who have helped refresh my memory with dates and factual information.

To the many people we met who helped us during our 1979 visits to Guadalcanal, Peleliu, and Okinawa.

To my Army buddies who have assembled on that heavenly parade ground of peace and love.

LeRoy B. Bronemann, PFC
Formerly attached to the 454th Amphibious Truck Company
United States Army (1942–46)

Incidents portrayed are accurate.
Names have been changed where necessary.

Acknowledgments

Combat photos were reproduced from U.S. Marine Corps photos, U.S. Signal Corps photos, and U.S. Navy photos. They were released by GSA National Archives and Records, Washington, D.C.

Contents

List of Illustrations xi

Foreword xiii

Preface xv

Introduction xvii

    I. New Caledonia 19

    II. Guadalcanal 29

    III. Pavuvu 51

    IV. Off to Peleliu 55

    V. Back to Pavuvu 81

    VI. Off to Okinawa 85

    VII. Okinawa Landing 91

    VIII. Mail Call 105

    IX. Pacific War Ends 115

    X. Typhoon 123

Presidential Unit Citation 133

454th Amphibious Truck Company Roster 135

Appendix

Introduction to Appendix 139

Preface to Appendix 143

Noumea, New Guadalcanal 145

New Hebrides 153

Guadalcanal—1979 154

Trip to World War II Battlefields 162

Our Trip to the Tetere Area 170

New Guinea 175

Peleliu 180

Koror 195

Okinawa 198

Illustrations

I: Map of New Caledonia 23
        View of ammunition and fuel explosion 26
        Second view of explosion 28

II: Map of Guadalcanal 30
        South Pacific seashell cross 45

IV: Map of Palau Islands 57
        First Marine Division on D-Day 58
        Amphibious craft landing on D-Day 59
        Marines taking shelter 60
        D-Day on Peleliu 61
        Aerial view of Peleliu on D-Day 63
        Supplies being transported 64
        Marine standing on Japanese tank 66
        Marines landing on Peleliu beach 67, 69
        Marines moving along Peleliu beach 69
        DUKW floating 75
        Wounded on Peleliu 78
        Mass on Peleliu 79

VII: Map of Okinawa 92
        Assault troops landing on Okinawa 93
        Aerial view of invasion ships off Okinawa 98
        Loading DUKWs 102
        DUKW crossing Bailey Bridge 103

VIII: Harbor installations 110
        Rifle sights lined up outside Okinawa cave 111

Illustrations

Introduction to Appendix:
    Author by foxhole 139
    Dog tags 140

Appendix:
    Map of South Pacific. 155
    Monument on Guadalcanal. 156
    Entrance to campground 158
    American cemetery on Guadalcanal 159
    GI-built road 160
    Rear end of a DUKW 161
    Corroded DUKW 162
    Road leading to Lungga Beach 163
    Foxhole 164
    Monument on Bloody Ridge 165
    Control tower at Henderson Field 166
    Red Beach 167, 168
    Remains of an American bridge 169
    Koli Point 170
    Sergeant Major Jacob Vouza and author 172
    Sergeant Major Jacob Vouza and his wife 173
    Abandoned amtracs 174
    Communication from Palau Museum 179
    Airstrip in Peleliu 181
    Monument on Bloody Nose Ridge 184
    White Beach, Peleliu 185
    Entrance marker 186
    Welcome sign at main dock on Peleliu 189
    School building 190
    Site of 454th Amphibious Truck Company 199
    Yomitan Airfield 200
    Map of South Pacific 206

Foreword

In this, his first book, Bronemann depicts the life of a GI who was drafted at the age of twenty-eight years as a private into the U.S. Army. He was discharged three years and four months later, still a private, proving that a man of that age has formed his own set of ideas, which cannot be changed or manipulated by officers—commissioned or noncommissioned.

During that time, he served with the 454th Amphibious Truck Company, which was attached to the First Marine Division for combat, and participated in two major Pacific invasions.

Despite the many obstacles confronting him, he tries to relate his experiences in a factual, yet entertaining manner.

In 1979, Bronemann and his wife revisited the areas in the South Pacific where he had been stationed and fought. Their findings after thirty-five years are interestingly chronicled in the appendix.

The card below is the reverse side of one appearing on the cover. It was used as an introduction to the many natives, residents, and visitors whom they met, and who so willingly helped them on the various islands they visited.

Lillie & LeRoy thank you for helping make our story possible. We have come to the Islands to refresh our memories.

"ONCE UPON A TIDE" is a So. Pacific story of action, humor, & adventure with a historic past.

This is LeRoy on Okinawa in 1945. The So. Pacific sea shell cross was conceived on Guadalcanal and was made throughout the war. Besides rings, watch bands, and necklaces, it was one of the few homemade "up front" war souvenirs that combatants sent home.

Lillie & LeRoy Bronemann
Box B
Fall City, Wash. U.S.A. 98024

xiii

Preface

Becoming a soldier doesn't automatically drape a superman's mantle over one's shoulders; neither does it guarantee brassards, or for that matter, even a lousy stripe.

Time and tide wait for no man. War is a tirade of philosophies that engulfs both single individuals and entire cultures. Air supremacy may have been the ultimate factor in World War II, as compared with the War of 1812, when a freedom-of-the-seas war was fought.

Many cultural and economic aches and pains pervaded the societies of Germany, the United States, Great Britain, France, and their allies. The reorientation of these social problems by Adolf Hitler ultimately involved the world.

The American armed forces awakened the islands as one would grab a sleeping giant by the hair. With an electrifying jolt, the twentieth century pulsated throughout the South Pacific. Every GI became an ambassador of good will. Children, women, and men who came into contact with them were befriended: candy for the children and women, smokes for men and women. It was indeed a gesture of friendship to share with those who were not familiar with an abundant way of life. Such actions were also rewarding; the friendships often blossomed into trust which was compassionately expressed by natives.

No enlisted man will read this book without recalling similar incidents and experiences that balanced the chafing from discipline.

Emotions change at the sight of a uniform. Old GIs reflect on their spent youth, with its attendant vitality, which boasted accomplishments of love and travel. A uniform is a mantle that cloaks many personalities; when nourished and disciplined together, however, these personalities reflect their combat team. It stirs an indomitable pride in all of us.

There is no greater moving force than a call to arms, to fight for one's country. No matter what the cause, the individual's soul becomes his country's emissary. He does as he is told. When things become difficult, the Marines are called. When a distress call becomes but a whisper, and the Marines are up to their armpits in trouble and mud, a miracle unfolds when the supporting forces of the Army, Navy, and Air Force provide their assistance.

A cause becomes an obsession. In numbers there is strength. Disliked and unpopular individuals, heretofore reluctant to pull their load under excruciating circumstances, will often rise to the occasion under combat. They then receive the most coveted title ever to be conferred on a fighting man—buddy. That singular and nonassuming word encourages friendship in spite of status, religion, or color. That title has a warmth that I hope you appreciate and feel as you read this book. Thanks again to my old 454th buddies who helped make my story possible.

Introduction

O<i>nce upon a Tide</i> is a story covering the problems, frustrations, and fears that plague the life of a combatant. High tide on D-Day was set as the time for invasion. Time marks the event; students who study history have another date to remember.

I actually began writing this book after the war, when I was asked by local organizations to speak about my wartime experiences. I wrote several condensed chapters on which I based my speeches.

* * *

My goals for this endeavor were to inform people about the comical and serious experiences encountered by the typical GI, and to apprise former GIs of the present conditions of those South Pacific islands.

I had always considered myself an industrious worker. During the Depression years in my hometown of Fall City, Washington, I worked for a bulb farm for thirty cents an hour. From the daffodil fields, I moved on to the Weyerhaeuser Company sawmill as a locomotive driver.

Simultaneously, I was attending the University of Washington, where I received a B.A. in economics and business administration in 1938. Within two years, after passing a civil service examination, I was appointed to the position of postmaster of Fall City.

I was very happy with my life. I had completed school, and with it, the accompanying financial demands. I was assured of a steady job and had just built a new house with the expectation of getting married.

My contentment was to be short-lived. It was during my second year as postmaster that Pearl Harbor was attacked. I was preparing for the Christmas rush when a friend walked in and informed me of the jolting bombing. I understood the consequences; my life would soon not be my own.

I attempted to join the Navy as an ensign by filling out an application at Seattle's Sand Point Naval Air Station. However, this pursuit was negated after I ignored two requests to join the Democratic Party. I was eventually drafted as a private into the U.S. Army in August 1942 at age twenty-eight. I had been an ROTC cadet at the university and been honored with a sergeant rating. Since only a commission as an officer would have served my ego, my self-esteem was shattered.

The politics of war meant little to me, except that I never liked to see a bully throw his weight around. I never feared the unknown—people of the highest caliber would always come to my rescue. Once in the armed forces, I was disappointed to see my college friends become commissioned officers while I, who was carrying a portfolio as a postmaster, was denied such a privilege. It has only been since then that I have discovered that both commissioned and noncommissioned officers experienced the same good and bad times.

— Chapter I —

New Caledonia

L eaving behind my loving family, including my parents and aunt, I headed for basic training at Camp Roberts in California. Once there, I was indoctrinated with discipline. Officers demanded that recruits salute them on every confrontation. They taught us that instead of working with people, we were to tell people. Telling people became a hobby for loud sergeants who knew every command and who exercised their vocal cords on weary draftees.

However, there was one gentle pat on the back that could have changed my entire Army career. It came as we broke basic training camp for reassignments. Captain Hooper came up to me, grasped my hand, and said, "We've enjoyed having you, son. Good luck to you no matter where you go."

When I went with several of my fellow Camp Roberts trainees to the Army Postal Battalion assignment in New York City, we arrived at the Hotel Breslin at Twenty-ninth Street and Broadway. After checking in and being assigned a hotel room, we assumed that a new role was beginning and that at last we could work along the lines for which we were best suited.

Next, we checked for mail. Imagine my amazement to find an airmail letter, transferred from California, waiting for me from the Aircraft Warning Service in Seattle, stating in brief, "Take this letter to your commanding officer for immediate transfer to the ACWS in Seattle, Washington. A master sergeant rating is waiting with a commission available in the foreseeable future. Signed, Captain, Aircraft Warning Service."

My knuckles were immediately announcing my presence at my company officer's door. On being invited to enter, I saluted as thoroughly taught in basic training, stated my rank and name, and followed with the reason for my visit. (This formality alone should have earned me the granting of my request!)

Undoubtedly the officer was unimpressed. Chewing on his cigar, as if he even hated it, he asked in an authoritative voice used to bully subordinates, "The Army sent you here, didn't it, private?"

"Yes, sir," I replied.

"Then you're staying. Dismissed."

I assured myself that had my letter been received in Camp Roberts, I would have had my request granted.

After a stint in the Army Postal Battalion in New York City, spent meeting some of the nation's brightest postal employees, I was replaced by a WAC and transferred to Moultrieville, South Carolina, in order to learn how to operate a DUKW—an amphibious truck.

From my later assignment at Camp Stoneman, California, we finally sailed for the South Pacific. Leaving California, our ship zigzagged across the Pacific Ocean in order to leave no traceable wake for enemy submarines. This maneuver took seventeen days. There were countless hours of lying topside under awnings spread over the ship's rigging—for some relief from the burning sun. Food was not bountiful, but that was inconsequential as most of the men were nauseated—only one step away from the miseries of seasickness. A few crossed the line and leaned against the ship's solid railing in an attempt to relieve themselves, often with no result, as their stomachs were empty from not having eaten a sizeable meal for days. A typical lunch was an apple and a sandwich.

It was customary to have boat drills on evacuation, in case of such an emergency as a hit from an enemy torpedo. All machinery was stopped; even the screw propelling the ship slowly died. Air no longer poured through the vents into our hold. Stagnant air soon caused the men to break into sweat. We would stand lined up behind the closed door, down the stairs and to the far ends of the compartments, ready to rush topside—waiting for the alarm or the pending impact of a torpedo. There were rumors of a submarine having been sighted earlier, thus adding to the pressure that this drill could possibly be the real thing.

Noticeably, our first sergeant was always in front. If he happened to be in the middle of the group at the start of the emergency, he slowly worked his way to the top of the stairs.

"One hell of a display of bravery, Sergeant!" was a taunt that did not seem to faze him.

During one of our drills a group working as a team decided that the sergeant should be deprived of his number one place on the stairway. One of the team members lined up beneath the stairway, while other men waited at the top of the stairs. At a given signal, the man beneath the stairway, armed with a pole, was to punch the sergeant in a sensitive place. The two musclemen were then to force him down the stairway, where, we hoped, he would be trampled to death by men determined to reach topside. However, no such emergency ever arose, and the sergeant's life was extended to cause added miseries to our Army lives.

Each night at eleven o'clock the ship's coxswain would pipe the crew. The microphone would click and the captain's deep resonant voice would boom out the order, "Doomp the garbage!" Although the microphone would then be turned off, the soldiers aboard would pick up the order and, with a striking degree of mockery, repeat the order one by one until the crew carried the garbage to the rail and properly dispatched it to its watery grave.

Every GI gave one order his personal attention, and that was the order to put out the smoking lamp. There was no smoking topside after this announcement. It was strongly impressed upon everyone that a match could be seen five miles away and would alert any enemy ship or submarine. For a smoke, the only place to go was below deck. For many, this was too confining; everyone preferred sleeping topside with only a blanket from his bunk to lie on. Some even gave up smoking for the night.

It was a daily practice to look for excitement, but seldom did we see anything. A few ships were spotted—but at such distances that they meant little to us. Telegraphers of ships would sometimes carry on Morse code conversations with lights.

Flying fish would often dart out of the bow wave and fly for fifteen seconds. There were often debates as to whether they flapped their fins to keep airborne or to glide. It was resolved that they were particularly adept at sailing through waves moving in their traveling directions.

At night the topside watchers often saw phosphorous water. It was noticeably light and often resembled the old phosphorus-illuminated watch dials.

Speculations as to where we were going, when we would arrive, and what we had to do kept everyone busy. Ironically, the true answers to these questions often contradicted the rumors. Letter writing to families, sweethearts, wives, and girlfriends spread throughout the United States also occupied many idle hours. Time for meditation led to the recording of sober thoughts. Home ties were strengthened and often a weekly letter was written, even though our letters couldn't be dispatched until we docked at some port.

That first port turned out to be Espiritu Santo, New Hebrides, where the ship's captain stopped to unload supplies. (It was a lonely, empty port with no buildings, no people, and no facilities.) An hour's shore leave was granted, leaving various sergeants in charge to see that the men were all accounted for and back on the ship in the allotted time. We walked through a grove of lemon trees and decided that we had reached that time in ocean travel which brought about the disease known as scurvy. Fresh fruit was therefore a must, and we shook one poor lemon tree free of its crop.

After reboarding the ship, we left for a place known as Noumea, New Caledonia—the land of the French, as we were soon to find out. We could finally mail our letters to the States!

On October 17, 1943, our company, the 454th Amphibious Truck Company, set foot on Noumea, New Caledonia. An amphibious truck company has fifty trucks that will take to water like ducks, hence the name ducks. In the Army they are each known as a DUKW.

A DUKW can haul a two-and-one-half-ton load from the water and then take to the highway like a regular truck without a single mechanical alteration—except for the disconnection of a propeller shaft.

Approximately 200 men belonged to a company. They were grouped as drivers, assistant drivers, maintenance men, and headquarters. Each group believed that it was overworked and underrated.

For twenty-seven months, the battle lasted as a friendly feud between the various groups, and between the individuals. Stripes mattered little in the friendly "digs" that passed from day to day. Humor was found in what the men said and did, for we were soon isolated from all the world—isolated as are men in a prison. Our prison walls were the boundaries of our island shore.

Our camp was located on the side of a hill. Steps had been cut into the hillside, and one climbed the hill as if he were going upstairs to a bedroom. Dirt that seemed resistant to the elements held firmly in place for our six-week stay.

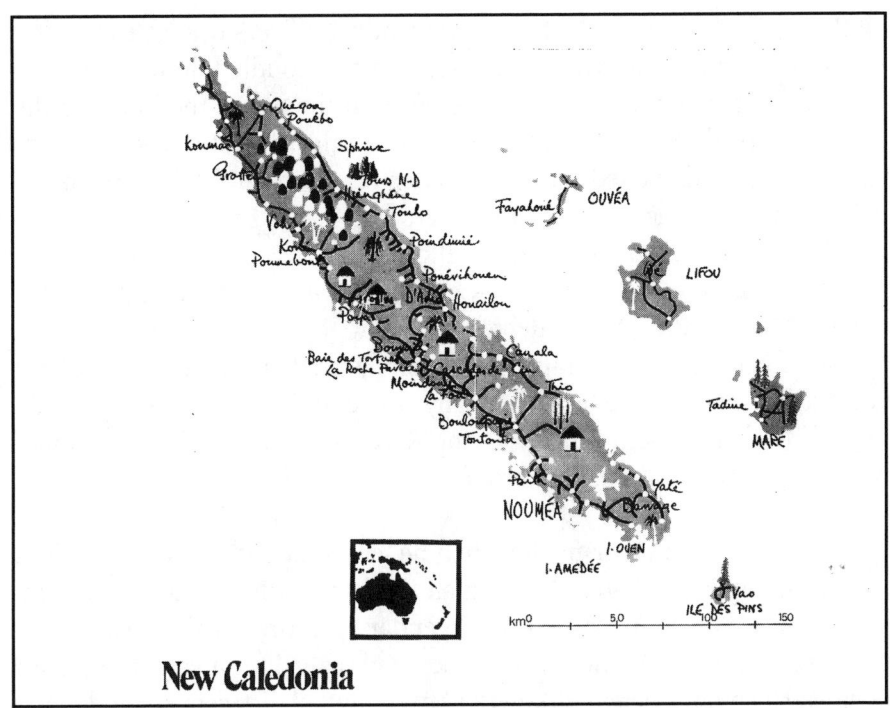

Map of New Caledonia

It was here that a lesson in discipline was taught. A sergeant, displaying the customary bravado of not giving a damn regarding his obligation to
repay a ten-dollar loan, was approached after our first payday.

"Sergeant," I said, "You promised to pay me the ten dollars owed me
since we last were paid in the States. Since we were paid yesterday I thought
you'd like to pay it back."

"You know, I forgot all about you and sent my money home," replied
the sergeant.

"That's a hell of a way to repay a loan, when you promised to pay it
back the next time we were paid. This is the second payday since you borrowed the money, and I want my money," I emphasized to him.

"No way," said the sergeant with a shrug of the shoulder, as if to imply
that a private was indebted in some archaic way to the higher echelon of
the Army noncommissioned officers.

"Look, I've come to collect the ten dollars. I'm going to beat you to a
pulp or drop dead trying if I have to. I'll kick, push, shove, or roll you right

off the top of this hill down to the commanding officer's headquarters tent, where you can explain why you are reporting," I loudly told him.

My challenging, piercing voice rang from the top of the hill over the rows of tents like a rooster's crow resounds in the crisp stillness of a barnyard court. Heads poked out from under tent flaps and from out of entrance doorways. Sleepy GIs got on their feet.

"I'll give you three minutes," I bellowed.

"Just a minute, just a minute—Sergeant Malino, Sergeant Malino, loan me ten dollars," shouted my debtor.

Within a matter of minutes, ten dollars were delivered to me! "A loud voice will always get you by in the Army," once commented an Army buddy named Brothers, whom I met at Camp Roberts, California. The ten-dollar bill stashed away was positive proof.

* * *

There is a lull in a man's life when he feels that nothing worthwhile is being accomplished. After checking all the latrines in the pubs to be sure that the walls or doors carried the legendary greeting, "Kilroy was here," the boys found little work to do. Work details called for men at the Eighth General Hospital, where buildings had been built of dirt, cement, and grass, and at the Twenty-ninth General Hospital, where buildings had been constructed of prefabricated materials. Nickel Dock often had work parties of fifty or more of our men, working in the naval supply area.

Maintaining our tent area on the side of the hill required the policing of paper wrappers, cigarette butts, and empty bottles, which somehow filtered into camp despite the fact that no passes were issued. Each meal was looked forward to with great anticipation; the cooks took pride in preparing a tasty, wholesome meal. With the excellent rations they could perform feats worthy of an Army citation—compared to their later despairing efforts, which degenerated in direct proportion to our advancement to the war zone.

It was customary for some to buck the chow line. This term referred to squeezing into the line up near the serving window so that one could be fed before those men who patiently waited their turn. Such actions brought verbal reprimands from those who brought up the rear of the line. However, no discipline was ever taken against the offenders. Why did I ever feel it was my noble assignment to correct this flagrant practice?

A fellow T-5 truck driver who was over six feet tall, and who weighed 198 pounds, made the mistake one night of bucking the chow line ahead of me. Because of his size, my subconscious mind immediately labeled him a bully. Adrenaline poured into my bloodstream, flooding my anger with a fight attitude worthy of a beer parlor brawler.

"Look, Johns, you're not eating ahead of me! You can break the line behind, but not in front of me," I emphatically stated.

"We'll see about that," he replied, taking no corrective action. He continued his collision course by staying in front of me.

My fighting instincts, previously indoctrinated at the University of Washington, were urging me to tear the man to pieces. I was measuring him for speed and strength, and was looking for signs of previous encounters such as broken nose, cauliflower ears, or missing teeth.

After he dipped his silverware and mess gear into the hot soap water and again in the hot rinse water (a practice that assured us of sterile mess gear), I duplicated the procedure and then took his gear from him. Laying both our eating utensils on a lister bag (a fifty-gallon canvas bag with four small bottom outlets for water), we started the fight.

It was nearing the end for Johns when someone grabbed my right arm. Looking around, I saw I was being forcibly restrained by a second lieutenant. Before I had a chance to say or do anything, my left arm was firmly gripped. When I turned around, I was looking at a first lieutenant who was smiling a pleased but not approving smile.

"Just what is the meaning of this?" he asked.

"I'm trying to tell T-5 Johns he's not eating ahead of me," I replied.

"That's right," agreed Johns. "I'm eating right behind him."

The line moved right along, but the whole company felt the impact of the chow line bucking episode; in the days to follow, the practice ended. The next day, however, a notice on the bulletin board reflected the captain's vote on the fight's outcome. As sole judge of the bout, he reduced T-5 Johns and T-5 Bronemann to privates! There was neither a win nor a draw, but the price of discipline was twelve dollars a month. That was the most expensive meal I ate in the Army, since we were never to receive a similar rate again as DUKW drivers.

* * *

Hobbies in the Army are profitable. Boys in the maintenance crew, who had at their disposal a choice selection of tools, were turning out metal wristwatch bands for fifteen dollars. These replaced our leather bands, which were deteriorated and rotted from sweat and exposure. For ten dollars they would turn out a monel metal ring. Many girls at home were thrilled to receive a ring made "just for you."

Probably no other hobby was as profitable as that of making necklaces, bracelets, and later my South Pacific cross from seashells. It all started when we first landed on New Caledonia. Much of our leisure time was spent along the seashore, where shells abounded. Everyone picked them up, although the ambition to make something of them was postponed. With the leather punch on our jackknives, some of us painstakingly drilled holes through the gathered shells and strung them on elastic strings.

From our hill outside Noumea we were not too far from a lagoon where we could swim or gather seashells. One Sunday, I took off to explore on my own. Arriving on the beach, I found some very nice shells. I felt that there would obviously be a bountiful supply of even more luxurious and beautiful shells on a distant island. This thought kept flickering across my brain, as I mentally calculated and recalculated the distance.

Finally, with a confident decision, I took off my clothes and started swimming toward the island. After twenty minutes, I began to feel tired.

View of explosion of ammunition and fuel at Nickel Dock, Noumea, New Caledonia.

The island looked as far away as it had from shore. I looked back toward shore and it appeared as though I had swum a half mile. As I was neither an experienced nor a long-distance swimmer, I began to realize that I was in trouble. To compensate for my misjudgment, I lay on my back and tried to conserve my energy. With each mouthful of water I tried to separate enough air to keep me going.

I subsequently turned around and headed hopefully back to shore. My arms and legs felt tired. Exhaustion made my ribcage hurt, for I was taking in air by gulps because I didn't want to breathe again; the waterline was getting above my nose. It seemed as though I was to be the first casualty in my outfit. My poor judgment was to be my undoing.

While the thoughts of drowning were taunting my weary muscles into delivering just another kick of the leg or a pull of the arm, a swish-swish sound caught my ear. Instantly, another evil thought crossed my survival-oriented mind—the possibility of being attacked by a shark.

"I can't, I can't, I can't fight a shark," I mentally repeated to myself. In my weakened condition I could only hope to curl up and pray it wouldn't attack. I then turned to face the sound of the swish-swish, and saw two airplane auxiliary fuel tanks gliding across the water. They were held together by boards, and were bolted in front and back and twice bolted in the middle, resembling an ingenious catamaran.

"What are you doing out here?" asked the man who was propelling the craft with an oar.

"Please help me, I'm drowning. Please," I pleaded.

I was pulled aboard and thanked God for being delivered. I then asked my rescuer how he knew I was in need of help. "I saw the splashing way out here and decided to find out what it was," he replied.

Our mutual curiosity made him my hero, as he certainly saved my life. If his life was spared in the Pacific war, and he should read this, I offer humble thanks to this buddy for saving my life.

* * *

It was a sunny day. The 454th was lined up to sign a payroll that would be presented through the proper channels for payment. While we were taking turns at signing, someone shouted, "Look at that puff of smoke!"

It soon ballooned into a monstrous cloud that hung over the city of Noumea, as it spread a little to the left and south of us. Speculations as to

Second view of explosion of ammunition and fuel at Nickel Dock, Noumea, New Caledonia.

the cause were bandied about; our officers later received a call for a larger work crew to report to Nickel Dock.

When we arrived, crews were working with machinery loading trucks with drenched supplies that were partially burned. The explosion had set the warehouse and dock on fire. As the dock was cleared of debris, a special Seabee detachment was tearing up and rebuilding the dock. It was a masterful bit of engineering, and GI savvy had the dock back in operation in a matter of days. While working that night, our crew came upon additional bodies that had been killed, either from the explosion or the fire that followed.

Nickel Dock was declared an off-limits area to all civilians. The cause of the explosion is maintained in closed files. Only the grim realization that these were the first dead Americans we were seeing impressed this indelible tragedy upon us.

For the balance of a month we did manual labor in the various Army ration, fuel, and ammunition dumps, awaiting the move to our next destination.

— Chapter II —

Guadalcanal

Shortly after Thanksgiving we were on our way to Guadalcanal. The heroes of the First Marine Division had been given a leave and were in Australia. So we were among the first pioneers on that island.

No newspapers heralded our arrival. Conversely, our arrival was shrouded in silence. Mail censorship was practiced. What the Marines had done was now a legend. Landing August 7, 1942, they had battled the Japanese to a stalemate—the latter withdrawing their troops February 1–7, 1943.

Our DUKWs were kept busy day and night bringing ashore rations, ammunition, airplane motors, wings, and fuel. During our leisure hours we washed clothes and pulled extra duty by building showers and latrines and digging drainage ditches. A can of gasoline placed under a grill served as our stove for boiling our clothes; a five-gallon coffee can was our wash-tub. We were issued mosquito bars to put over our cots so that mosquitoes couldn't feed on us while we were sleeping.

Souvenirs were the most highly sought commodity on the island, as there was nothing to buy. There seemed to be no community life nor any visible social group. There was no store—not even a place to buy an ice cream cone. We were on a desolate island where GIs had to make the most of an isolation that bordered on prison confinement.

There was a work force composed of Rennell Islanders who worked for the British Command. These men were of slight build, and of rather short stature—averaging five feet two inches in height. They had tattoos on their faces and all over their bodies. They brought with them many beautiful seashells, which greatly intrigued all of us.

The Marines had already bought and traded in seashells and shell necklaces, so the natives had a set price of five cents a shell or twenty dollars a necklace, the latter of which GIs soon learned to make. A matching necklace and bracelet set, at twenty dollars, seemed a bargain since it was the only souvenir available for stateside girlfriends, relatives, or acquaintances.

Shortly thereafter, a sign appeared on one of the tents: "South Pacific Traders—Pvt. Brecka—Pvt. Bronemann." No business was ever transacted but the tent became a hotbed for bull sessions and beer busts. We rallied the Southern GIs, trying in vain to have them secede from the Union so that we could join them and return to civilization under the pretense that we were secessionists! A great morale builder, it was good for many laughs— with the Southerners justifying a century-old war that had been fought over 7,000 miles away.

New Caledonia had served as a getting-acquainted camp for those of us who had gone through school in Moultrieville, South Carolina, learning to operate our amphibious trucks. Guadalcanal became our school for producing and delivering the goods. We were designated to haul supplies from cargo ships, anchored off shore, to the appropriate sundry dumps. We soon learned where food ration dumps were located, where the clothing warehouses had been built, and where ammunition was to be stockpiled.

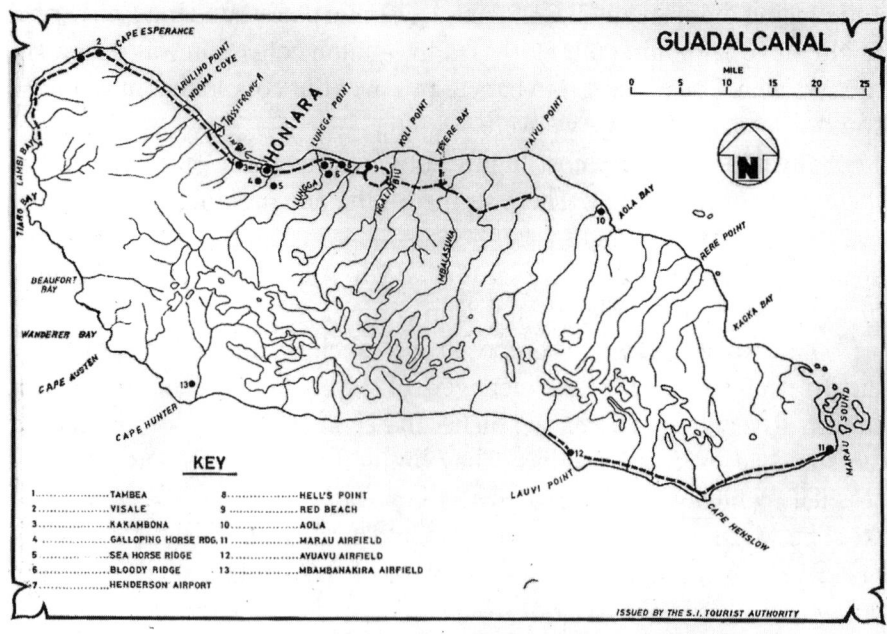

Map of Guadalcanal

The accepted order of a DUKW driver and his assistant driver was broken up. The rated DUKW driver was ordered to drive the vehicle twelve hours daily, and the assistant was ordered to relieve the driver for the twelve-hour nightly shifts. Our tonnage figures soared. We were building a colossal depot for all future Pacific operations, and drivers competing for records found they could bring ashore as many as twenty loads in a twelve-hour shift. Our contribution to the war effort was at last being made.

Our 6 A.M. and 6 P.M. meals were eaten at camp, but the midday and midnight meals would leave our company area by truck at 11 A.M. or 11 P.M. to be hauled approximately fifteen miles to Koli Point where we were working. Thus, the drivers always had a hot meal. Time was saved and more work was accomplished. Round-the-clock operations were proceeding efficiently, and our commanding officer discovered that he had a company of men who could deliver the goods as well as get into trouble if temptation crossed their paths.

While at Lungga Point hauling Australian cargo ashore, it was rumored around that we soon would be hauling fresh meat. Immediately there was a release of gastric juices, turning the DUKW drivers into pirates craving grilled rib steaks. Instead of delivering the goods to the Australian camp, two DUKWs found their way to the 454th mess hall. Our officers, always informed by those who curried favors, dealt harshly with the offenders; extra duty was assigned.

"Ya know," said one driver, "it's hard to steal, but it's agony to see meat that I stole being served at our mess hall, while I sweat digging a latrine!"

Extra duty consisted of filling foxholes, painting DUKWs, and digging out stumps.

On guard duty one night, when one couldn't see his hand in front of his face, I decided to sit in the officers' jeep behind the officers' tent, and planned distracting and disturbing noises so that they couldn't get their sleep. Soon I started imitating a cat. "Meow-Meow-M-E-O-W-Meow-MEOW—M-E-O-W."

Finally, a glimmer of reward—a GI shoe came flying out of the tent. I was enjoying a warm sense of achievement and a long inner chuckle when the cat wailing began again—only this time I wasn't producing it. With hair standing on end and voice box choked to emit not a sound, I was paralyzed by a frightening scare as a real purring cat jumped from the ground into my lap. I would have walked my post after the experience if only I could have kept my feet on the ground. Where that cat came from on Guadalcanal no one will ever know.

* * *

Christmas was approaching, and a suitable gift for the most deserving woman in the world was the uppermost thought of every GI in the outfit. Upon arrival at Guadalcanal we had found different types of shells—the golden ringer and the cowry shell, as we soon learned to call them. Since seashell souvenirs were the only commodity for sale, it followed that everyone settled on a necklace—bracelet set for mother, wife, or girlfriend..

Ned was a skilled jeweler who already had made a set. He had the tools, wire, and rubberized electrical tape needed to pack the shells. He was engaged by several men before I had enough money to order a set.

"Glad to do it. Will get at it this week," agreed Ned.

A week passed and I didn't receive my order. Another delayed promise of next week was offered. After a direct confrontation he came up with a compromise.

"I'm not feeling well, but I'll show you how, and you can make your own necklace and bracelet," he volunteered.

Jewelry work is a slow, fastidious, and painstaking occupation requiring steady hands and some degree of control over profanity when disaster occurs. After three days of breaking wire from twisting too hard, and breaking shells from tamping the packing too tightly, patience and persistence rewarded me with an eight-shell bracelet. Now I had only to put another twenty shells together for the necklace!

Trial is a teacher of sorts and, by trial and error the necklace was assembled. It was thrilling and rewarding to send my mother a homemade necklace and bracelet set. In due time I was appreciatively thanked and told how beautiful it was. Mothers are a man's best ego builder, so I concluded that I was on a par with the Marines, natives, and any other seashell artist inhabiting the South Pacific.

A visit to sick bay, in order to have a growth burned from my shoulder with nitric acid, brought about my initial involvement in the seashell business for profit.

"Can you lay out a necklace for me?" asked the corpsman.

"Come over to my tent at noon, and it will be done," I replied. His pleasure was evident as he beamed at the sight of the perfectly matched shells forming the necklace.

"Beautiful," he said, and added, "How much?"

"Nothing," I answered, "unless you might be able to spare a fifth of sick bay alcohol."

"You'll have it tomorrow night after I get off work," he promised. We parted friends, both highly pleased with our bargains, since neither of us had a cent to our names. Cash transactions seemed a ridiculous gesture of stateside formality.

One hundred eight proof sick bay alcohol is indeed John Barleycorn corked in a bottle. Made of grain, it is nonpoisonous, thus assuring any GI that it was drinkable. One bottle of alcohol will make two bottles when it is cut with water in equal proportions.

By a coincidence, six free bottles of Pepsi-Cola were issued to each man in the outfit that very day. This was our first issue since we had arrived on Guadalcanal, and a three-month thirst was hard to quench. After drinking a third of the contents of our Pepsi bottles, a light shot of diluted alcohol was added. Tent mates and visitors nodded their approval, smacked their lips, and warmed up to the occasion by admitting that Army life did have some fringe benefits.

"Where else can you get free Pepsi and free alcohol?" "Have another shot!" These and other statements were quickly uttered. One round of drinks was followed by still another.

Undetected, a mechanic from the maintenance crew left our tent and reappeared when our first alcohol bottle registered half full. He brought with him two other mechanics, holding thirty dollars in their hands.

"We'll buy the other bottle for thirty dollars," one said. Quick glances passed among our tent mates.

"Thirty dollars for the half-bottle. We know where we can get more," said one tent mate. It was an outlandish bootleg price, but the transaction was quickly consummated.

Visitors from other areas of the camp gathered in our tent as the cheerful attitude hit a crescendo that climaxed in singing patriotic songs. Only after having finished our second bottle did we break up the party and snuff out our candles for the night.

Life without anything to look forward to grew quite dull. Working around the clock was the rule except when severe storms became a risk for the equipment. As one driver put it, "We're expendable, but it's damn hard to replace a DUKW!"

Australian beer (ale as they called it) was the next temptation that only the devil could have encouraged newly chastised drivers to use. It was February and the weather was as hot as haying time back in the States. We happened to be hauling Australian ale, so the drivers made it a point to bring some home after an international episode.

An armed Australian guard was assigned each loaded DUKW as it came ashore. As the night wore on, the temptations multiplied in direct proportion to our thirst. We felt as if we were dying from dehydration. In desperation, one driver said to the guard on his DUKW, "Don't you Australian blokes believe in treating your English cousins to a drink of ale?"

"Was wondering why we couldn't be social about this," he answered. Consequently, to use a limey term, he forthrightly opened a case.

The two men proceeded to enjoy their beverage. Its high alcoholic content soon had them in a slightly intoxicated state. Next, they avowed they were buddies. Soon they were greeting the others with hail-friend gestures as they waved their ale bottles. No recrimination entered their minds— their sole mission was to put the Australians and the Americans on a permanent ally basis of winning the war together.

Other drivers and guards soon became intoxicated with this binding-together philosophy, along with the contributing aid of additional cases of ale. When the curtain finally fell on this international high-seas comedy, our company officers searched our vehicles and found fifty-four cases of the best ale that ever came upon the island. We were threatened with a court-martial but received company punishment instead.

Returning to our camp for a visit several days later, one of our Australian cousins was asked about his punishment. "What did your officers assign you to do for punishment?" he was queried.

"We were taken back to camp and were told, 'Go to bed, soldiers; sleep it off,'" was his surprising reply. A new era of military independence was born. We liked the democratic attitude of our Australian comrades, thinking of them as super soldiers, who were not greatly affected by superiority of rank.

We returned their visit one Sunday to find their camp in utter turmoil. The atmosphere was festive. War was something of a bygone era—a day when King Arthur turned to his Knights of the Round Table for noble deeds.

Runners were warming up for foot races. Windows had been set up and were now staffed by competent tellers who took bets on the various runners. Posted on a signboard were the race numbers, and the names of the runners in each one. It had all the markings of the Kentucky Derby. A favorite in three of the ten races to be run was a captain. He evidently was an outstanding athlete, since he was competing against the best of the rugged Australian enlisted men.

We lost touch with these good friends as we moved up the line, but some of their names found their way into my buddy book.

* * *

Our company punishment for stealing the ale consisted of removing the dirt that covered Marine-made foxholes. They were located in the perimeter area of Henderson Airfield and had been prepared for its defense. They were super bunkers. After removing the layer of two yards of dirt on each foxhole, we came to a roof of coconut logs. The logs were sawed in two, placed in the bottom of the foxhole, and then covered with dirt in order to return the area to its former condition. It was a reclamation job that removed some of the jungle war scars around Henderson Airfield.

It was a steady four-hour grind with a noncommissioned officer standing over us as a guard. Only ten minutes of rest were granted during each hour. No water was given to us except during our breaks. Water was most essential after working in such heat. After pulling two hours of extra duty, Bise said, "Don't know what the hell has happened to me. I was brought up in a Christian family, went to church, then I'm drafted; next I'm paying for my wayward ways with the U.S. Army prosecuting me!"

The work was humiliating and the day was beastly hot. Sergeant Malino, smoking a cigarette while sitting on a log, moved himself to the shade of a coconut tree. Leaning against the tree, he said, "Time for a ten-minute break."

We took off for a warm drink of water. Taunts and comments greeted us both leaving and returning to our work area. "How do you like your landscaping job?" "Any gold in them thar foxholes?" "Tell Malino to knock it off in the heat of the day." "This heat isn't fit for man or beast to work in."

Rube Prop from Georgia had been to a doctor the day before and was given a light duty slip. In the course of light banter, Brian Greg from Maine happened to notice Prop working silently by himself. "You look sick, Rube," said Greg.

"I am," said Prop sitting down. "Got my papers to prove it." Whereupon he went through his billfold and produced the medical certificate issued by the doctor.

35

Two men fainted under the harsh command of our sergeant. Kusker was suffering a heart ailment and became the first victim. Shortly thereafter, Hutton suffered sunstroke. Prop went to the medics after the day's extra duty, and the doctor took timely steps to safeguard his health.

After the extra duty, those men scheduled for regular duty were transported to Koli Point, where we were loading the first Marines for their Pavuvu Island encampment.

Early in the evening drivers complained to our beach sergeant that the winch operator on board ship was unnecessarily careless in handling the cargo we were transferring from our DUKWs to the cargo ship. Sergeant Cris went on board the ship and complained to the head officer. No correction was made. The operator evidently could still reach the bottle from which he was drinking, for his actions became more uncoordinated.

Steve Ors and I had just sent a big case of equipment aboard, and were waiting for the straps to come back so that we could attach the second case and get away from an accident that was bound to happen. The operator swung the hook over the side in a wild, meandering arch. The fourteen-foot strap slipped off the hook and disappeared into the darkness above the ship's light, which was blinding as we looked up at the ship's top deck from the DUKW.

With a crash, the strap came hurtling out of the night's darkness and went through the shatterproof windshield of our DUKW. As it swung through, some part of it struck my forehead and the bridge of my nose. It caused my legs to give way and I fell into the cargo compartment. Not wanting to frighten my coworker, I gathered my strength to stand up in order to indicate that I was all right. My coordination failed me; I could not stand, but I could support myself on my hands and knees.

Arriving at the Marine aid tent, my senses were numbed to the point of answering only simple questions. My repeated request that I wanted only to sleep was granted when I finally passed out and was carried to a tent.

The following day at noon, I heard a voice exclaim in subdued tones, "He's still breathing." It was Cris, who had come to visit the man whom he considered was to be the first casualty of the 454th Amphibious Truck Company.

Returning to our company with my head bandaged, I was given a break—I was not on extra detail anymore; neither was I ordered to drive. Bending over made my head ache, and I would often black out. The bridge of my nose was swollen and sore, and as it healed it caused one of my nostrils to emit a whistling noise on exhaling. Later they termed this a deviated nasal septum. A catch in my neck prevented me from turning my head completely to the left, and as my head healed a bad scar remained over my right eye. The blow had nearly crushed my skull and had almost broken my neck!

* * *

Food was becoming a choice of either Vienna sausage in tomato sauce or Spam. Cooks tried to conceal the identity of these basic meats by preparing them in various forms. Often the resulting concoction was relegated to the garbage can by the GIs. Occasionally, the sauce was more delicious than the meat dish.

A gifted salesman, Sergeant Miles pulled a few drivers aside one day and informed them with great secrecy that a shipment of fresh chicken was to be cooked for our Sunday meal. "Why not volunteer for mess hall duty, help in the kitchen, and enjoy the extra fare we will prepare for the occasion?" he seriously suggested.

Breaking a cardinal GI rule, the drivers volunteered. At last a break with the mess hall sergeant. A curried favor, a gastronomical breakthrough—it was a picture of the original Pilgrims' Thanksgiving.

Sunday came and the willing attendants added table decorations to supplement the anticipated chicken banquet. The frozen Australian chickens were cut in pieces and were fried with batter in deep fat, much as Colonel Sanders might prepare a delectable chicken-in-a-barrel treat. Miles was putting his southern reputation on the line.

The meal was served. Soon the diners started tasting the beautifully browned and delicious batter. Some men then tried cutting the chicken with no success; some tried chewing it from the bone with no success. One man, with extra gusto, pulled so hard that the drumstick slipped from his grip, and the elasticity of the tough meat caused it to snap back in his face!

"It's the only meal I ever ate where I was bruised by the meat," commented the diner.

"Where in creation did you ever get this rubbery chicken?" asked another.

Red-faced and embarrassed, Miles tasted his cooking to discover that the taunts were justified. He promptly dumped the entire lot in the garbage, following the example already set by the early diners.

There was no explanation for the toughness of this chicken except that the meat was lean and dark in color, suggesting that it was perhaps some kind of wild bird slaughtered and sold to the armed forces as choice chicken.

* * *

The USO center on Guadalcanal evolved slowly. Later came the order to put screens around our latrines and showers, for nurses were coming. It caused endless excitement, and for once we looked forward to seeing a woman as a child looked forward to seeing Santa. The rumors of nurses did not materialize, unless it happened after we left the island.

It was late February. The mosquito menace was at its height, for below the equator the seasons are reversed. Jolly Robers, with murder in his eye, decided to cremate the many mosquitoes that collected on his mosquito bar. He lit a newspaper and when it looked like a flamethrower in action, Robers started waving it back and forth in front of his bar. Everything was going fine until a part of his newspaper came loose and settled on its top. A good fire had started before Robers realized his mosquito bar was burning. A drowning person couldn't do as much thrashing around as did Robers in putting out his fire.

McCuster had other ideas on how to do away with ants, mosquitoes, and termites. He prepared a solution of stove oil, insect repellent, and gasoline, with which he drenched the floor of his tent; he then tried spraying it with DDT. Having finished, he relaxed by climbing on his cot. Unfortunately, the smell irritated his nostrils, so he lit a cigarette. Unmindful of the results, he repeatedly flicked his ashes on the floor. After he put out the fire, he said, "I thought the sun was getting damnably hot!"

A spark had ignited the gasoline and had burned one corner out of the tent. He covered that corner with a blanket so that the officers wouldn't notice the damage.

One hobby developed by the boys was the fermentation of raisins into a concoction known as raisin jack. Boverich and Corporal Beck were the winemasters until Beck was seriously hurt during the battle of Peleliu and had to be evacuated.

Boverich and Beck had opened five gallons of raisin jack and were having a party. The third time Boverich went to fill his canteen, he noticed that a thieving GI, referred to as a rat, had removed part of the contents. "Corporal Beck, Corporal Beck," shouted Boverich, "a rat's been in our vino puro."

Beck, with a rapidly stiffening tongue and obviously willing to share with the four-legged kind, answered "Did he drink much?"

* * *

After four months, the drivers were improving their driving abilities. Moving a thirty-foot-long vehicle between coconut trees, without touching either the front or the back of the DUKW, was an experienced maneuver. Pulling the DUKW exactly halfway alongside a tree, and then making a turn, would give necessary clearance as the rear end would swing away. Practicing this clever maneuver made the drivers look like pros on land.

To maneuver properly alongside a harbor cargo ship, a technique was devised by the drivers who had long ago lost their rating, and who couldn't be chastised any further for any dents they added to the abused hulls of our first assignment vehicles. This maneuver was to drive the DUKW at full throttle straight at the cargo ship as if to ram it broadside. When it appeared that inertia would carry the driver to the boat, he would cut the power and give full rudder right or left, depending upon whether he wanted to come alongside starboard or port. Calling ourselves Coast Guard commandos, we soon learned to maneuver at sea with amazing deftness, often bringing smiles to the faces of many able-bodied seamen who rode our DUKWs for an island visit.

"Want a beer?" asked Prop one day after cleaning and painting the hatches and cargo compartments of our DUKWs.

"Heat's got you," was the reply. "Where on a scorching day like this could you come up with a beer?"

"Right here," he said, as he pointed to the rear hatch of his DUKW.

We all looked and saw nothing, then added, "Want a fat lip for being funny?"

"Not joking," said Prop in a reaffirming tone. "Take another look by dropping into the hatch!"

Once down in the rear hatch, you could see the single case of beer sitting on top of the gas tank, which was located on the right side of the DUKW. It was the only case of beer not removed when we had had our Australian beer bust. This proved to be the only safe hiding place on a DUKW—a secret our drivers shared with no one! Subsequent searches were made of our DUKWs, but never again were we to be caught with another case of beer!

* * *

Payday came, and with it the usual rash of poker and crap games. Unless the money was sent home, it was lost to those men who were knowledgeable about the games and who, in turn, sent not only their money home but ours along with it.

I was always willing to learn, but my first lesson was a disaster. Receiving fifty-five dollars for a month's wages sounds like a miserable pittance when taken out of context. One must remember that we were clothed, fed, and cared for by the sergeants and officers, who served in a paternal capacity, making sure we were comfortable and happy. In addition, we were getting a chance to see the world!

These positive arguments will be repudiated by many enlisted men who solicited the services of a chaplain, sought the help of a higher-ranking officer for some redress, or wrote to their congressmen to stop a complete reduction of liberties by officers who soon elevated themselves to capacities of demigods.

Having accepted my humble pay of fifty-five dollars, I was anxious to turn my earnings into a hundred or even a thousand dollars, as were many GIs. With canteens of raisin jack at our elbows, with our shirts off and with cigar smoke curling past our noses and into our eyes, six of us sat in Boverich's tent playing poker. Payday always found us with plenty of money and with no place to spend it, thus all of us could afford to gamble. As we hoisted our cups and felt alcohol flowing through our blood, our bravado increased as our gambling judgment decreased. After two hours of playing I was a spectator, for as a participant I was broke. As a sideliner my verbal annoyances distracted the players from concentrating on the game.

I had lost my month's wages, but did I worry? Did anybody need money? I reasoned that one needed it only to gamble. Thus, I proceeded to borrow my next month's wages from a buddy who was the big winner at the time, and who gladly loaned me the fifty-five dollars on credit. I slapped to death my share of mosquitoes in Boverich's tent that memorable night, as I lost next month's pay!

I was convinced that I was a dummy for having initially played poker, and a fool for having tried to recoup my loss. I was not only broke, but would have no money next payday. My financial cloud was indeed enough to shut the sunshine from my life for a long time.

As the evening passed and the liquor disappeared, a funny butterfly feeling in my stomach told me that neither the liquor nor the gambling was agreeing with me. A most miserable night was spent by alternating convulsions of my stomach and my mind. My stomach was trying to rid itself of poisonous liquor and my mind was trying to rid itself of the debt I had incurred.

The next morning Boverich came over to see me. "You need a little snort to settle your stomach—come," he convincingly said.

I followed as he led me to a place where he had hidden a five-gallon can of raisin jack. When he took off the lid I could understand why I felt horrible. The fermentation of the raisins had eaten through the enamel on the inside of the can. Imagine my poor stomach.

Cal Smith had been the first man in our outfit to buy a piece of jewelry from an industrious Marine jeweler; six shells wired together resembled enough of a bracelet to justify his five-dollar expenditure. A high-pressure sales talk may have been involved in the transaction, which I observed. The Marine jeweler charged five dollars for six shells that he had acquired from the natives for five cents apiece. My mind was made up; I would become a jeweler.

Natives, like everyone else, respond to kind treatment. I had soon established myself as a casual acquaintance to inhabitants from all parts of the island. They all understood English and some could speak fluently. They came to me with their newly arrived brothers from the home island. They used the word brother to denote any male member of their island. He would lay out his shell collection and quote his price. His price might have been a pair of American scissors, a belt, a pair of trousers, a pipe, tobacco, or a cigarette lighter.

A few tricks involving the disappearance of coins used to strike these natives dumbfounded. Their native jargon would bring the whole village to the spot where I performed my tricks; I would slip the coin up my sleeve and in my ear, or would snatch a dime from their hands and simultaneously replace it with a copper penny. Their amazement led to my purchase of the best seashells, as well as of some beautiful inlaid work and carved pieces. To them I was the great white magician.

If I was to become a seashell jeweler, I needed more seashells, so I decided to walk to the native village. As was my custom, I left the company area to hitchhike to that desirable location. Once I arrived there, I noted the official KEEP OUT signs posted by the British Command. I crawled through the fence and was heading straight for my targeted location when

I heard the shouts of an Australian officer. During the time he questioned me about my business, my outfit, and where I was camped, I thought back to that old letter which started with "Greetings," and reviewed all the trouble it had gotten me into since I had been drafted into the Army.

As I answered him, expecting to be reprimanded or to have my company commander later do so, he seemed amused at my story and proceeded to show me the native handicrafts that he had obtained in his years of working around the islanders. Pudding bowls, replicas of sailboats, war clubs, walking canes, and combs, all inlaid with mother-of-pearl, were displayed. He explained that the natives who worked on Guadalcanal came from other islands, and only upon their arrival could one hope to buy the finest shells and handicrafts because all the GIs were ready buyers. Competitive buying was alerting the natives about our business methods.

I thanked the officer, took my leave, and never entered another native village.

* * *

I was indeed very disgusted and continued to berate myself for my poor judgment. I attempted to seek a way out of my financial dilemma. If only I could think of a way to make an attractive South Pacific seashell souvenir that didn't consume a day's work. I visualized a sterling silver pin with a cross attached to the bottom. With pencil and paper I drew a sketch and sent the idea back to my girlfriend in New York City so that she could implement this long-shot concept. It could be made of wood, plastic, or sterling silver, preferably the latter.

Miracles are performed by women, for within two weeks a sample was sent for my approval. It was perfect: sterling silver properly engraved "So. Pacific," with a neat loop made on the bottom of the bar and with a self-locking pin clasp on the back. Beautiful!

Confronting this enterprise was an obstacle comparable to swimming back to the United States, and that barrier was the price of $135 for a hundred pins. This news was a low blow to an entrepreneur who was already hanging on to the ropes. The monetary battle literally had me on the mat for a full count.

How could a man raise $135 plus pay back the $55 he had borrowed in the poker game? Like a true business tycoon, I ordered a hundred pins with a sweetheart's promise to pay promptly on delivery. Love, blind as it is, could plainly see the futility of raising the money.

Time was running out on our Guadalcanal stay as we received orders that we had been attached to the First Marine Division for combat and were to join them on Pavuvu.

This was cause for a drinking party, a discussion of feelings, and the establishment of a new common denominator that would cement the drivers into a close-knit group of professional operators who had a fellow driver's welfare as our first concern.

"We need some sick bay alcohol, and you know where to get it," said the speaker of the group who came to my tent.

"Yeah, we liked it," said another.

"Wow, what a wallop it gives," remarked the third.

The fourth man only grinned.

"Do I look like a bootlegger?" I answered.

"No, but you can get it, and we've got the money," replied the spokesman.

"Money!" A dollar sign crossed both pupils as my eyes bulged with a new radiance of hope. I could see myself not only out of debt, but making enough profit to pay for my hundred pins.

"I'll see the man tomorrow," I quickly replied.

After my sick bay call the next day, I casually asked my corpsman friend the cost of one gallon of sick bay alcohol. "It costs eighty dollars a gallon and you have to take five gallons, as it is easier to take it off the inventory in five-gallon lots," he informed me.

Back to the boys.

"Ya mean, we have to raise $400?" asked the sergeant.

"Right."

"Jeepers," said another with a whistle through his teeth. "Here's a hundred and sixty dollars—go demand two gallons."

My return trip with $160 got me nowhere. The corpsman was on a five-gallon lot of easy money and didn't want his profit lowered. "Go back to your outfit," he said, "and raise all the money you can."

My second effort was an additional eighteen dollars from the temperance league, who only drank rarely so as not to become addicted.

"This is it," I said on my return. "One hundred seventy-eight dollars is all the cash our whole outfit has. Even men with A-1 credit ratings can't borrow or beg any more bucks than you're looking at. It's been a long time since payday. Please give me two gallons."

He slowly took the cash and quietly put it away, whereupon he went into a storeroom and returned with a five-gallon can of alcohol. "I can handle this on the inventory easier—take the whole can," he muttered.

He nearly ruined my life. Not that I ever had aspirations to buy or sell booze, but my conscience confronted all the moral precepts painstakingly taught to me over the years by my parents, my school teachers, my minister (who also served a dual role as scoutmaster) and my elocution teacher, who was the local doctor's wife. What if they ever found out? Their innocent, hand-molded, model young man would indeed be socially ostracized.

To antagonize the situation, I was leaving the sick bay just when the show finished at the Coconut Log Theatre. Hurrying through the company area on my way to the Henderson Airfield bomb dump, approximately two city blocks away, every headlight on fifty vehicles seemed to spotlight me.

"Just punishment," my conscience said, "for being such a black sheep."

Only after safely hiding the five-gallon can did I slip back to my tent for one of the most restless nights' sleep I have ever had. Surely a murderer must die a thousand deaths for the life he takes. This was truly the lowest and most distrustful thing I had done since I was thirteen years old, when my father caught me smoking cigarettes stolen from the hired man, beat me, and put me to bed in the middle of the day.

Financiers are very demanding, especially when they want to get on with their party. The following night five one-gallon vinegar jugs were emptied of their contents and with a trusted buddy I proceeded to divide the spoils. "One thing we forgot is a funnel," I quipped.

"Don't need one," he said. "I've got a brand new packet of condoms in my wallet and I'll never use 'em. We'll cut the end off one and stuff it in the bottle; the other end will slip over the opening in the can."

Not a drop was spilled.

"Here's a gallon for you and your buddies—a repayment of eighty dollars; here's a gallon for the sergeant and the mechanics—a repayment of another eighty dollars, and here's a gallon for my tent, which will take care of another eighty dollars," I said, as I separated the three gallon jugs.

The thought quickly ran through my mind that for only three gallons I was realizing $240. Only $128 had to be reaped from the last two gallons and my total financial catastrophe would be overcome. No more money nightmares; I had won the battle with the Yankee buck.

The South Pacific sea shell cross. The pins were made in the States and the shells were attached while moving through the war zone. Fourteen hundred of these were made from Guadalcanal to Okinawa.

Ned, my original necklace jeweler, was now going to sick bay complaining of muscular aches and pains. His lackluster attitude caused a feeling of deep sympathy in my heart for the kindness he had shown by teaching me the art of making seashell jewelry. When he pleaded for a gallon of white lightning, my bird-in-hand business practice flew out the window. He walked away with the only smile he had mustered in weeks. That smile was the sole pay for Ned's gallon, since he promised the eighty dollars next payday.

Arriving at his tent, like a lion who had made the kill, he was beset by virtually all the alcoholics in his area. There was much celebrating, and as the eye of this cyclonic drinking storm gathered momentum, Ned was blown from his feet and landed on his bed in a drunken stupor. Some claim he never sobered up until he reached the hospital. The doctor's diagnosis of malaria sobered him up. Malaria—the first case in our outfit—had to first hit the man who owed me money. Ned was evacuated to a separation center and was on his way back to the States.

* * *

Black and bleak hung the money cloud. With a financial problem and with only one gallon to provide the answer, one reviews his mistakes. Plagued by poverty! It was a lifetime nightmare. Insufficient money necessitated working my way through the University of Washington. Then there was graduation, and good luck smiled on me only long enough to assure me of a permanent job with the Postal Department as postmaster in my hometown of Fall City, Washington.

Emboldened with this start on a postal career, I had talked my father into loaning me enough money to buy an estate being probated by a customer who was trying to get "even a small cash amount." As I thought about these events from my past, my mind continued to wander.

Depression days had put a knot in the purse strings of buyers. Cash was hard to get. A house plus five lots cost me only $1,200. With my postmaster's job plus the rental from the house, there was a light at the end of the tunnel that urged me to build another house. Carpenters were available for 50 cents an hour. Again Dad moaned when confronted with a loan. My mother hurt me when she pointedly asked, "Are you trying to break us and cause us to lose our home?"

Borrowing the money had truly been the hardest part of building the house, for within the year of 1940 it was completed. As a new house it rented for twenty-seven dollars and fifty cents a month. This caused an aunt to ask, "Why do you rob those poor people with such a high rent?" The depression had really altered everyone's value of a dollar.

As I continued to reminisce, I recalled that my basic training campaign closed with a company show and a twenty-five-dollar savings bond being offered as first prize. In addition to doing a declamation piece taught by my elocution teacher, I was asked by Private Harold Bord, then of Los Angeles, to be part of his show, which was a takeoff on basic training. The two of us were a comedy team equal to Laurel and Hardy. My commands were shouted; his stoic reverse executions panicked the hilarious GIs and brought belly chuckles from the front-row officers.

For a grand finale, our slapstick Army comedy called for an inspection of his rifle and dismissal from formation. After inspection, he was dismissed, whereupon he did an about-face and clobbered me with his rifle. Helping me to my feet, he was again ordered to attention. As his noncommissioned officer I gave him a good report on his rifle inspection and for a reward, extended his weekend pass to a month's furlough, whereupon he pretended to faint. This brought down the house. Bord won the coveted prize that should have paved the way to a movie contract for him.

The later untimely meeting with the New York Company officer, which pre-empted the previously mentioned ACWS transfer and possible commission, was just another example of my continuous bad luck.

Hence, that is why I eventually arrived in Guadalcanal suffering from both empty pockets and a defeatist attitude. The fruit I reached for was always at my fingertip but never in my hand.

* * *

I was subconsciously reliving this past, when reality hit me with a voice asking, "Who has alcohol for sale?"

It was Beck, an old American infantryman left over from the Guadalcanal invasion who had joined our outfit. "You're in the right tent," I quickly answered, "But I need something to put it in, as I only have a gallon left."

"Fill up this stubby. Say, buddy, haven't you gotten your case of beer yet?' he added.

"What beer?" I asked

"Everybody in the whole company is being issued a case of beer up at the orderly room," he informed me.

A case of beer for each soldier was the biggest issue of beer we had on Guadalcanal—just as we were about to leave for Pavuvu. Empty bottles were being discarded like empty cartridges being ejected from a machine gun.

Beck's suggestion of filling up a beer bottle—half with water and half with alcohol—was a good one, and in no time the beer bust ended with a five-dollar competitor!

My last gallon of alcohol was stretched into the most appreciated word in a debtor's dictionary—solvent.

As promised, the first two South Pacific pins arrived in an envelope and were put together before we left for Pavuvu, by immediately attaching a shell cross to each one. These readily sold for five dollars apiece.

Visiting the cemetery on Guadalcanal one Sunday, I counted twelve hundred crosses. I resolved to make a seashell cross for every one of them.

The acquisition of seashells was always a problem, however.

Consequently, five hundred seashells were purchased on Guadalcanal to take care of the young business that was to become the choice of all combatants sending home souvenirs. In fact, it was the only souvenir labeled "So. Pacific."

Thanks to Lillie (now my wife), the idea conceived on Guadalcanal was to become not only a remembrance but also an outlet for the pent-up frustrations of many GIs who later helped make the souvenirs, collect the shells, and even sell the finished product. It was a hobby made possible only because Lillie was one girlfriend who willingly made sacrifices of her leisure hours, after putting in her eight- to ten-hour days working for the New York Central Railroad.

No previous work I had ever done called for such artistry. It was an idea that appealed to every GI. Its novelty sparked many ingenious ideas and original workmanship.

Mack, who lived across the company street from me on Guadalcanal, became notorious for having supplied the First Marines' oxfords for their leave to Australia after their year-long battle. When we had just arrived from New Caledonia, our dress shoes only took up space in our duffel bags. Mack offered us ten dollars a pair, which was an amazing offer, and the deal was quickly closed. Gullible Marines, in their anxiety to be well-dressed when they arrived in Australia, gladly paid Mack twenty dollars!

From shoes to moving meat from Australia was an easy step for Mack since he was able to pay cash for the meat. He was supplied with a jeep and became involved in some questionable negotiations. His downfall came when he sold pictures of our girlfriends to the natives. Our company captain dealt harshly with him for this unscrupulous practice and set out to correct him with company punishment. His peculiar behavior came to the attention of the sergeant, who oversaw his punishment and recommended that Mack visit the hospital.

Our whole company was shocked with the next report on Mack. He was caught on Henderson Airfield impersonating an officer, wearing a doctor's uniform with a major's insignia and demanding a flight back to San Francisco for an emergency operation he had to perform. He was flown back to the States, but the treatment was for his own welfare!

It was just before we left Guadalcanal that one of his tent mates received a letter from him in which he apologized to all for the silly things he had done to disgrace not only himself but the Army. Caustic remarks indicated that he was the only smart man in our outfit—at least he had made it home!

It was our buddy Mack who had thought that my idea of the seashell cross was so wonderful and that he could sell them for five dollars. I was now beginning to question the fine line between genius and insanity.

* * *

During the spring of 1944 our DUKWs went through extensive maneuvers. One-hundred-five-millimeter guns were fired from the DUKW when the vehicle was approaching land. Our company was attached to the Fortieth Division for combat. New Ireland was the island to be taken.

Something went wrong with the plans, because we were soon back on our old schedule of hauling cargo for the island command. June 1944 brought us the good news that we were assigned to the First Marine Division. At last we were going to see combat!

Pat Gray, postmaster of Cary, North Carolina, agreed to take my place in the island command, where I had been transferred to do payroll work. My legitimate excuse was that I came here and wanted combat since that was the only way to win a war—fight!

Secretly I realized that I had to be up front where the action was if I was to sell my pins. The finance officer, Service Command APO 709, was the man who officially approved my return to the 454th Amphibious Truck Company.

Was it hard to leave Guadalcanal? Ask the men who listened to the hundreds of parakeets squalling at dusk; ask the men about their endless battle with mosquitoes, flies, and the countless Atabrine pills forced on them to prevent malaria attacks.

There was the creeping feeling of loneliness, and when the Marines loaded out and left pet dogs behind to howl in the moonlight, it was an eerie feeling of doom—doom that became pronounced with the firing of a shot that ended some dog's life. Truthfully, those kindest of pets were blessed with the easy way out, as we look back on the blackest day of our war years.

On Monday evening, April 2, 1979, after revisiting old campsites near Henderson Field, Guadalcanal, thirty-five years later, I was prompted to write this bit of philosophy:

So wide and blue is the Pacific
With countless coasts for the tides to pound,
One ponders at the wonders of its watery life
And the clash of philosophies heard the world around.
There is enough salt in the ocean
You need not shed a tear,
Battle sweat from combatants
Paid for the islands before your visit here.

— Chapter III —

Pavuvu

It was a short sixty-mile ride from Guadalcanal to Pavuvu on an LCI. Our whole company, except for an advanced detail, was crowded on the small craft in an unventilated hold that forced most of us to ride topside.

"God, look at the reception committee," piped Prop as we came in and dropped the ramp on the beach. The reception committee turned out to be enthusiastic Marines rooting for the winning ball team, which was helping pass an otherwise dull Fourth of July on Pavuvu.

"Drivers," shouted Malino, "get off the LCI and drive your DUKWs back to camp—follow my jeep."

Interest in the ball game exploded like a Fourth of July firecracker. We proceeded to curse the Army, Malino, and the day we were born.

Our motor pool was in a coconut grove down a badly rutted road ideal for extra-duty assignments such as picking up coconuts. Amtracs used the same roads, cutting them up deeply. It wasn't many days before the heavy rains made the roads impassable for our DUKWs, so a channel was dynamited through the coral reef, and our DUKWs took to the water the back way.

After we had parked our DUKWs that Fourth of July, we carried our personal effects from the motor pool to the brow of a hill, which was to be our camp for some time. It was a quarter-mile walk with our packs, foot lockers and whatever else we had had on our vehicles. Upon arrival we found our tents neatly dumped in a pile by the advance party.

"Get 'em up, get 'em up," shouted Malino.

Five members of our group hurriedly pitched a tent, while Big Stoop Burkie and I agreed to carry up two cases of beer we had hidden on our DUKW. As we sat around our tent, dirty and sweaty, enjoying a beer in the heat of the day, a couple of stray Marines came walking by, passed the

51

tent, looked in as they passed, and then wheeled and came back. It didn't take us long to learn that a fifteen-cent stateside beer was bringing twenty dollars a case, or one dollar a bottle!

The second unbelievable event that shortly followed was the order to draw mattresses. We later learned that since we were attached to the First Marine Division, we were a branch of the Navy and thereby entitled to use mattresses. Life was looking rosy!

A theatre screen was directly behind our tents. Coconut logs served as seats. Our first evening at the theatre was the beginning of our disillusionment. As the first reel started unwinding, the usual hush fell over the interested moviegoers. A lush harvest moon added softness to the setting. A light sea breeze gently tossed the coconut tree palms in a typical lovers' setting. It was almost as if Hollywood was preparing such an enchanting moment. Then it happened. A defective celluloid broke and the machine shut down while an amateur projector operator tried to fix it. Back in operation again, the first reel soon finished. Then came another delay—a very long delay.

"What's the matter?" shouted one of the boys.

"We're waiting for a jeep to bring us reel two from down at Steel Pier," shouted back the operator.

Two shows were shown the same night—no wonder the celluloid broke. During the lull the boys got rowdy and rough, wisecracks and jovial laughter made the rounds, and flashlights played on the screen.

"Quiet," shouted one of the soldiers. "Who do you think you are, a bunch of Boy Scouts?"

"Quiet yourself, soldier," shouted another voice, "even if you think you're a Scoutmaster!"

It was not long before the moon disappeared and a heavy rustle of the palms told us that a squall was on the way. The less romantic audience members quit the show and raced for their tents; the more enthusiastic stuck out the show despite the fact that the raindrops, beating against the palms, made the soundtrack inaudible. Crouching under ponchos and huddling together for warmth, we received good basic training for the foxhole life we were soon to experience.

"God, I can't believe it," said Prop one day.

"Believe what?" asked Milt Bore.

"Believe that we're going on a blitz September fifteenth. Why, I've been here a month and have done nothing but pull KP."

So it was! Some of the boys stayed in camp doing KP. The rest of the company was out every day landing the Marines on some new beachhead, and helping with the loading and unloading of their 37-mm guns. These dry runs were an easy day's work for DUKW drivers, as we reported to work at 8 A.M. and were back at camp by 6 P.M. We ate our lunch of K-rations in the field, drank coconut milk, and told our long stories of our year-old romances while the Marines secured their respective assignments.

Then came the final day—no more hunting for seashells, no more shows, no more idle talk. Sandbags were placed on the front of our DUKWs, completely covering our windshields. Three deep was the order. Three deep it was! We all safely smuggled our mattresses aboard our DUKWs—we weren't going to part with the comforts of home.

Jungle hammocks were issued. Maps were studied and then we were given the long orientation lectures about what we were to expect. A feeling of contributing to the war effort was at last a part of us. We were off for the Battle of Peleliu!

— Chapter IV —

Off to Peleliu

It was a short run down to Guadalcanal where a sham landing was held. I got to use the jungle hammock I was issued, and this was the first and last time.

We went to see our old buddies on Guadalcanal and told them where we were going so that they could take an added interest in their old outfit. We also helped them drink their beer, which was issued to them by the case. How different from our small trickle of six beers every two weeks on Pavuvu!

We reloaded our DUKWs on the LSTs. When the maw of the LST closed for the last time, our checking started. Everything was in order for the landing. Every Marine riding on a DUKW had his assignment. No one felt certain of his lot. Nothing was being left to chance.

The Marines were daily checking, cleaning, and oiling their guns, for around salt water guns need close watching to keep them from rusting. Lifeboat drills were religiously attended and blackout regulations were carefully observed.

We were heading for the equator and September 15, 1944, was set as D-Day. It was hot almost beyond endurance. A tarpaulin was spread on top of the deck to keep the sun off the men as they rode topside; no one wore a shirt. Small poker games were soon started; pinochle and casino were played by other groups.

For two weeks we lived on the LST, making the most of the long chow lines, for we were fed exceptionally well by the ship's cooks.

It was not long before Rabbit and I started making seashell necklaces and bracelets for twenty dollars a set. I was saving my money while Rabbit was losing his earnings by playing rummy with the boys. It was September 13 before I had rounded out one hundred dollars.

A crap game started in the crew's chow compartment the early part of one evening. It didn't take long to convert me from a spectator to a participant and from a participant back to a spectator. It was rough going.

The day preceding D-Day we started to gather our belongings. We laid out our one-piece fatigue suits, inasmuch as orders came that everyone should be fully clothed upon disembarking. That night we slept little. Our LST was not too far from our objective at midnight, for we could see terrific flashes of light in the inky murkiness that swallowed our convoy as it rode the choppy sea.

As we traveled in the direction of the flashes we imagined a gigantic naval battle in progress between our battleships and the Japanese Navy. As we closed in, it became evident that the island of Peleliu, rather than the Japanese fleet, was taking the beating from our Navy. That night was very tense as starry-eyed combatants lined the bow of the LST, speculating, speculating, speculating!

We were topside at daybreak. In the distance was Peleliu. It was lifeless and shrouded by a mist that quickly retreated with the sun's first rays. On the firing line lay the cruisers and battle wagons. Volley after volley went whining toward the mute island where soon we were to walk. It seemed incredible that anyone could be alive after the Navy's blistering assault.

A plane was seen over the island at medium altitude. Whether it was one of our observation planes, or an enemy's plane sent up to make a counter offensive, we'll never know; it came down in flames.

We were in for a treat at the chow hall—but the damned hotcakes stuck in my throat. The coffee couldn't wash it down, so I gave up without eating a thing.

Topside spectators were of the opinion that the Japanese offered no resistance. No shots were fired at us all morning; no Japanese planes came in to attack us. Circumstances indicated that our landing was to be a routine affair.

Combat in wartime is the degree of involvement! Newspapers cover the event, giving as precise an account as it is humanly possible to convey with words, pictures, and eyewitness description.

Ask anyone who has been through a war, and he will be the first to admit that the confusion, scope of activity, lack of communications, and isolation of units make the ultimate outcome a hazardous guess. Pressures

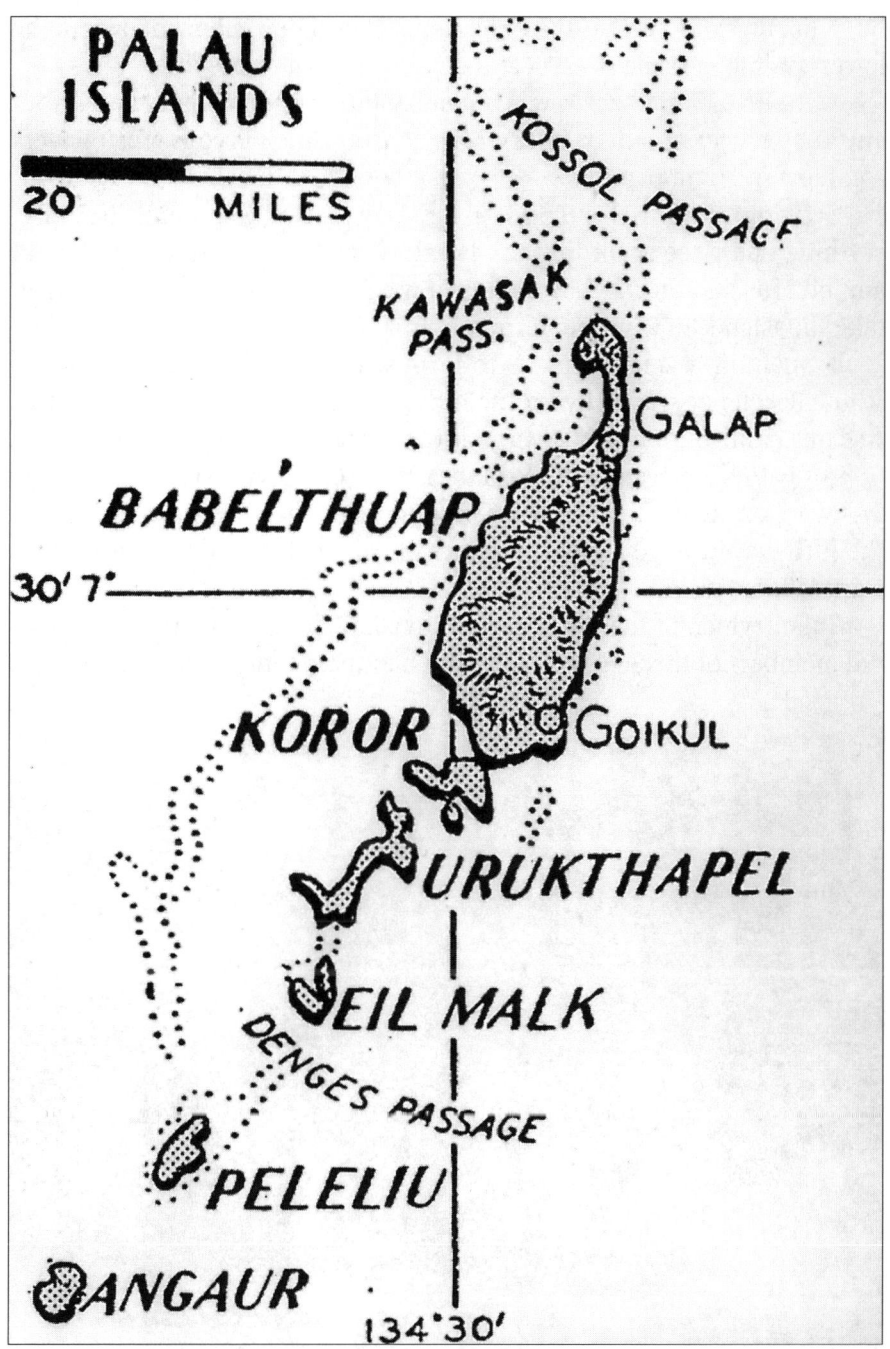

Map of Palau Islands

build up, tensions mount, and of necessity, men stoop and maneuver in the lowest profile possible to protect their bodies from enemy fire.

"Oh, my aching back," was a combatant's legitimate lament without any known back sprain or injury. Muscle strain and nervous tension were a combatant's companions.

September 15, 1944; 8:30 A.M.—D-Day, H-Hour, and high tide! Everything had gone according to plan. LSTs disgorged a steady stream of amphibious equipment that we hoped was, in a matter of hours, going to take the island. In a simple formation maneuver, all vehicles were to assault a certain beach, and were to form when their flag was flown. Our White Beach flag was to fly for the fifth assault on D-Day. At long last this was our contribution to the war effort, no matter the consequences!

Alligators and water buffalo of the amtrac category had made it ashore, and were on their way back for a second load when the signal ship gave the fifth wave the go signal. We were off in a column led by an LVP toward White Beach.

Infantrymen of the First Marine Division had nothing to say; neither did members of the Signal Corps, who had their communications system

Troops of First Marine Division en route from attack transports to beaches of Peleliu Island, Palau Group of Western Carolines on D-Day.

compactly set in a small trailer and loaded on our DUKW. Their minds were either rehearsing their duties or paying one last fleeting visit to the ones they loved. Some lit a last cigarette. One flicked out his cigarette lighter as if it were a match, then absentmindedly flipped it into the ocean.

The water started acting up, boiling along the shoreline. Near the beach, the water was splashing about as if a large school of fish was caught in a trap. As it turned out, it was the heavy enemy fire and the exploding enemy mortars that were causing the tumultuous water.

Seasoned Marines trusted the drivers and said nothing. This was no time for bull sessions—every man was left to his own thoughts. Our DUKWs pulled as close to shore as possible without running over any of the previous four waves of infantrymen who were still in the water seeking protection from the heavy small arms and mortar fire.

Burning DUKWs and burning amtracs told us that all the mortar shells weren't missing. Marines were lying behind a small coral shelf, making it impossible to drive our DUKWs on land. Whistling bullets bore down on us as we hit the water like rats leaving a burning ship. By now the front line extended twenty feet from the beach into the water!

Amphibious craft landing on the beach at Peleliu in Palau Islands, D-Day. A line of tanks and DUKWs is approaching the shore.

I could scarcely believe my ears when a buddy of mine crawled alongside of me and said, "You won't have any trouble with seashells here. That's all I see every time I duck under the water!"

Then it happened! Mortars were zeroed in on our loaded DUKWs, which were parked along the beach line. Hits were scored on four DUKWs in rapid succession. Drivers shouted to Marines, crouching beneath a DUKW for protection from rifle fire, trying to warn them that the next DUKW was loaded with explosives and flamethrower fuel. The good Lord spared this DUKW—the mortar fire ceased!

Marines were lining the beach as far as the eye could see. Some were crawling up the beach to dig holes in the sand; others were firing and hurling grenades. Eyeing a large stone pillar, I crawled and ran in a stooped position until it fully protected me from the front and left side.

Try collecting your senses when bedlam and death are shrieking around you in every conceivable voice! It was the fired rifles of enemy and Marines, mortar shells landing on us, and mortar shells fired by our troops. Our Navy guns were seeking out targets, adding to the firepower; mines exploded as amtracs climbed up the beaches. All hell was breaking

Marines take shelter under the stern of a DUKW on Peleliu while two other vehicles burn in the background.

loose; no ground seemed passable. Death waited to turn back any advancement.

A corpsman, answering a hit call, was in turn killed. Another corpsman started crying for the loss of his buddy. Cris slapped him back to his senses. "Get to your knees; keep down," the sergeants were shouting.

The two large rocks that extended twenty feet in the air, giving protection from the front and left side, were just close enough together so that by using my arms and legs I could elevate myself. As I did, the distance narrowed at the top so that it was then possible to force my body and my canteens between the rocks, allowing me to hang suspended with full use of both hands and legs.

Removing my helmet and putting it over the end of my rifle, I slowly raised it up to the top of the rocks and then a few inches higher so that if anyone was lying on top, it would dislodge him or bring a burst of rifle fire. Instantly there was a burst of fire, with several exclaiming, "We've got him!" An enemy soldier had been dropped to the ground.

D-Day, September 15, 1944—Peleliu. Entrenched Marines on beach. Vehicles in background were abandoned because the first waves of infantry were pinned down by enemy fire, and the vehicles could not advance without running over them. A DUKW burns in the background—twent-five of our fifty DUKWs were knocked out on D-Day.

While I was still up on the rocks, a sweeping view of the airstrip to the south revealed dozens of men crawling on their stomachs.

Bringing my rifle down, I replaced my helmet and was sighting my gun when a "Don't shoot" order was shouted, followed by "Our men!" It was a Marine officer protecting his men. How he ever sighted me and communicated with me, in that frightening moment of a man's first taste of horrifying war, was a miracle.

"Get DUKW 417 unloaded," shouted one of the radiomen on our DUKW. I hurriedly climbed down from my rocky fortress to help unload the equipment. With heavy lifting, eight of us managed to get the quarter-ton jeep communication trailer, laden with gear, up the side of the DUKW.

"Let her down," ordered the communications sergeant.

With a splash, the trailer landed on its side in the water and was hastily righted and shoved to shore.

Like firemen working to salvage a burning house, combatants were helping everywhere. "Get these wounded loaded and out of here."

A lowly private could have given the order, but its meaning and importance were obvious—ringing with the authority of a general. The order was promptly executed, as an amtrac driver with a fragmented leg was hoisted aboard; his alligator had hit a land mine. Laying my M-1 on the front of my DUKW, I hurried to assist.

Still trying to free himself of his flamethrower, a hapless Marine was helped out of his harness and over the side of the DUKW where he showed us his ground-off heel—a cleated vehicle had run over his foot as he lay in a foxhole pinned down by machine gun fire.

A redheaded Marine, shot through the chest and suffering from pneumatic thorax, asked to have his head propped up so he could breathe more easily. It was easier to lay his head on my lap. He repeatedly informed me to tell the medics he had been given morphine. As his senses built up, he would repeat the order.

Eight injured men were delivered to the aid station. It was no more than six pontoons lashed together with a Red Cross insignia for identity. Manned by a doctor and two corpsmen, it was an intermediate stop to stabilize the patients before their safe removal to a hospital ship.

Drawing alongside the aid station, we expected action, but the shock of seeing these wounded men immobilized the corpsmen. Finally, the

Aerial view of Peleliu on D-Day with beach head established. DUKWs and Amtracs leaving beach with wounded. After dropping off casualties at a temporary floating aid station, they returned to the battle with reinforcements, food, water and medical supplies. In the background is the airstrip.

doctor gave an order, and the corpsmen reacted with true professional efficiency. Our DUKW was promptly unloaded, freeing us for another trip back to hell's inferno where the caldron was still boiling.

"What in hell?" My rifle was missing from the front hatch—it had fallen off crossing the reef. I was fighting a war without a rifle!

It was around 10 A.M. when a formation of planes was observed coming from the northwest. It caused many a heart to skip a beat when they were first sighted. When no antiaircraft fire went up as they approached our convoy riding at anchor, we knew that they were on our side.

Peeling off, they came down hard and fast, machine-gunning and dropping rockets that had an eerie sound, as though death was being announced. One of our sergeants thought that the Japanese were firing rockets at the planes. Unloaded, they returned to the carriers.

There is no sound that cuts through your ear and paralyzes your nerve center as does a rocket. On release, it starts a whine that increases in

Supplies, ammunition and water are brought ashore on Peleliu after assault forces have pushed the enemy from the beach.

intensity until the piercing noise deafens you. The ultimate explosion is a relief, even to those of us who are on the ground. It was the only source of firepower that completely silenced the enemy. Five minutes would elapse before the Japanese regained their positions and started firing again.

We came alongside various ships before receiving orders to take reinforcements ashore. On the afternoon run, the shoreline congestion was still building, but DUKWs and amphibious tanks (alligators and buffalo) were moving freely over to the airport. A mine, half-buried in the sand, was visibly marked with a flag. Marines were crossing the field under heavy fire. While crossing, the Marines were beset by enemy tanks, which were hastily dispatched by our bazooka gunners.

With shells, mortars, rockets, and ammunition exploding in the most insane fireworks conceivable, one becomes awestruck. You wonder how those ground-tearing, tree-destroying missiles of steel can be missing you. A scream, a poncho-covered body, a bleeding buddy, a call for "medic"—these realities build an apprehension that death is stalking you every second.

Dig your foxhole deeper; move to where an artillery shell previously exploded—hoping no two shells fall in the same spot. It's like betting on a roulette wheel—into which hole will the ball bounce? You wait for the whole island to explode and slowly sink into the ocean.

This day of days would come to an end.

Clinging to the bouncing ball of life and facing an evening brings new confrontations. A scolding, fussing thrush sounds a forlorn note of discontent and contempt, for those who have so badly distorted her way of life. It is the quiet settling of gunfire that makes the evening seem like it is abounding with witches, cats, and vampires possessed with supernatural powers who move at night with exceptional ease. We unanimously agreed that the enemy possessed extra powers. They were so well acquainted with the island that it was like walking around in their bedroom—they could feel their way!

Anxiety mounted as probabilities were expressed. "Probably they'll have more tanks back in the hills." "Probably they'll get reinforcements tonight."

One rumor bounced around that we were all to evacuate the island so that it could be shelled and bombed some more to weaken the Japanese resistance. This rumor never materialized as the Marines kept slugging away.

Our equipment took to water the first night to avoid being hit or destroyed on the ground. Ors, driver of our DUKW, pulled alongside a barge loaded with ammunition that was to go ashore the next morning. For safety's sake the DUKW was driven into deep water for additional protection from the naval firepower.

Catnaps on the barge were disrupted as the audio and visual effects of a war were dramatically presented. Some heavy shelling from a battleship would light the whole lagoon as well as the island, like a sheet of lightning in an electrical storm. Traces from battleships in shades of red, green, and amber would carry across the sky. Flares from the infantry would light up the Peleliu airstrip. Machine guns and rifle fire prefaced the slow descent of the parachuting flare on which thousands of anxious eyes in the harbor were fixed. Marines in the field were hastily watching the terrain for the slightest movement, the slightest change in topography. It was a grim game of holding the line. Miraculously, morning arrived.

Although units had scattered, the second day found us regrouping on White Beach about 200 yards toward the airfield. Our DUKW losses on the first day had been twenty-five—our original full strength had been fifty DUKWs! Our company commander offered a word of praise for the work we had done on D-Day. "Keep moving reinforcements and supplies," he emphasized. "We'll rendezvous here tonight. Maintenance will try salvaging any vehicles not too badly damaged." This was the summation of the warmest words ever spoken to his hard-core drivers.

A hole had been torn in the Japanese defense of White Beach, permitting more maneuverability. DUKWs and amtracs moved with increasing confidence. More reinforcements were brought ashore, followed by rations, ammunition, and a cache of drinking water in five-gallon cans. A Marine guard was assigned to protect this water supply, indicative of its scarcity. As the temperature rose to 105 degrees, water was requested before food.

Coming ashore near White Beach on the second morning with a load of supplies, a Marine sergeant directed us to a company of black soldiers who not only needed the supplies but would unload them. Willingly,

A Marine stands on a Japanese tank. The Japanese made a disastrous tank attack on Peleliu on D-Day, only to be wiped out by American tank crews and bazookas.

Marines with tanks and amphibious vehicles landing on Peleliu beach, Palau Islands, D Plus One Day after heavy American naval and aerial bambardment. Taken from a carrier-based plane. Amphibious tanks and DUKWs in foreground, airfield in left background.

Marines with tanks and amphibious vehicles, landing on Peleliu beach, Palau Islands, D Plus One Day after heavy American naval and aerial bambardments. Taken from a carrier-based plane. Amphibious tanks and DUKWs in foreground.

67

several boarded the DUKW and proceeded to hand down cartons to those on the ground. Work was brought to a screeching halt when two artillery shells exploded in the vicinity. Everyone hit the deck expecting more, and there were more! One of the shells had set something on fire that was burning, giving off a heavy brown smoke that smelled like sulfur.

When somebody shouted "gas," panic and pandemonium broke loose and everyone headed for the beach and water. Authoritatively, an officer pulled his sidearm and ordered, "Don't move!"

White eyeballs rolled in every direction, but the officer was joined by a super-giant black sergeant who calmly said, "You all get back to work, hear?" He had confronted an explosive situation which turned out to be the only gas alarm ever given. Fortunately it was erroneous, as we were all caught without carrying our gas masks.

Heeding a plea for 75-mm canister shot for a Sherman tank, Ors found a supply. It was promptly loaded, and we and Sergeant Brown were hastily on our way to deliver it. Going north from White Beach, we pulled up, parking the DUKW on a small turnoff, while an effort was made to locate the tank.

Proceeding on foot through the scrawny brush, we found the tank located in exactly the only place it could take cover—in a clump of trees. Elementary warfare, I reasoned!

The lieutenant was duly informed of our cargo, for which he expressed his gratitude. Hurrying back to unload the DUKW, the lieutenant and I couldn't believe our eyes as we watched it hurry back out to the airport road and start back to White Beach with the sergeant hanging on the outside as if he were expecting enemy fire.

"Lieutenant, shoot the coward," I shouted.

But the lieutenant wisely replied, "Too many are dying—no use to aggravate the situation."

With a bitter feeling of failure of not having carried out our assignment, my long miserable walk back to our rendezvous area began. Anger had put a very cheap price on the head of one cowardly sergeant. While mulling over the apparent weaknesses of men, I became conscious of bullets passing over my head—whish, whish, whish—not too far, but too close for comfort.

The switch from anger to fear was compounded when 37-mm guns, manned by Marines, opened up at the other end of the airstrip. These

Marines with tanks and amphibious vehicles landing on Peleliu beach, Palau Islands, D Plus One Day after heavy American naval and aerial bambardment. Taken from a carrier-based plane. Smoke rising from burning installations in hill area in background. Amphibious tanks and DUKWs on beach in forground.

Marines moving along beach on Peleliu in Palau Islands after D-Day landing following heavy naval and aerial bombing. They are passing an upturned DUKW and tank.

shells were clearing my head with a whoosh, whoosh. My dilemma was obvious—I was caught in a crossfire!

Instinctively I hit the deck, crawling up to an abandoned airplane motor, where I lay partially protected until evening shadows gave me cover. This cooling period softened my vengeful hostility, making the confrontation with the sergeant a rational meeting. He explained that the Marines ordered them out of the area, fearing the DUKW would draw heavy enemy fire.

"You see," he added, "we were between the front lines of the Marines and the Japanese."

Toward the end of the day, just at dusk, a load of reinforcements climbed aboard our DUKW. They were headed for the front line. Circling the airstrip, we were stopped at a Marine command post. During a short dialogue between the command post officer, a major, and the officer of the reinforcement squad, a phone rang and the dialogue was interrupted.

"Repeat that," ordered the major. "I'll be damned," he commented, as he gave additional orders. "Don't try to replace him; we're sending you replacements." The major hung up.

Turning to the captain, who was his aide, he said, "We've lost our second observer on the high ground. Now we have to fight without observing our gunfire."

"I'll go," said the captain, as if he was volunteering to scout a basketball game.

My analysis of that captain's character was prompt and sincere. He was the world's bravest man!

"You will not," said the major. "We are not sacrificing men needlessly. We'll work out a solution tomorrow as our forces consolidate." Whereupon he gave final orders to the lieutenant on our DUKW, and dispatched us to the front lines with instructions to pick up a 37-mm gun left on the north end of the airfield.

We were off with the reinforcements, rations, ammunition, two Doberman pinscher dogs used to help detect enemy troops, and a supply of communications wire and equipment.

Greeting us was another officer, who came from behind a rock formation where Marine combatants were crouching and moving slowly, slowly, stealthily, in a circular pattern to a higher rock formation.

"Any water?" he asked.

"Yes, sir. Five gallons here, sir," was my reply.

Ors did not agree with me, repeating our preinvasion order of keeping a five-gallon can of water on the DUKW at all times. With a heated exchange of words, he and I were on a collision course when the officer intervened.

"Men, we have enough fighting on hand without a battle between ourselves. Forget the request."

He was showing intelligent leadership, as he could have given us a direct order to leave the water. I have often wondered at the wisdom of our actions that day, after faithfully following the instilled preinvasion order. We had delivered reinforcements to what later became known as Bloody Nose Ridge.

After we unloaded, darkness was making pockets of sinister and foreboding shadows. We remembered our orders to return a 37-mm gun from the north end of the airstrip. There is no reducing the size of a thirty-foot-long DUKW. We felt as conspicuous as a domestic duck in a tree, as we drove out on the 12,000-foot runway to look for the gun, knowing that every Japanese pillbox on the escarpment above the airfield had an open-curtain view of this seemingly suicidal gun rescue. With eyes and mind visualizing and concentrating on our objective, it came into sight as a welcomed prize. Once the tongue of the 37-mm gun was locked into our towing shackle, we were off in one wild dash down the runway.

Running without lights to eliminate conspicuousness, we hit bomb craters on the runway fast and hard. No 37-mm gun was ever given a faster or rougher ride. It was bouncing out of shell holes that often threw it into the air higher than the DUKW, but it was delivered to the command post. Dismissed, we were off to our predestined bivouac area.

This being the second night of combat and our first night together as a unit, we dug foxholes and settled down in pairs. No blankets were needed. It was one-hundred-degree weather. In addition, we were wearing impregnated coveralls which, we were told, protected us from lice, mosquitoes, flies, and other insects. A password was given to all.

Some opened a box of C-rations for a light snack, more out of habit than of hunger. A sense of togetherness and interdependency was pulling us into a buddy relationship, which dictated that your buddy's life was as important as, if not more, than your own. In these wretched holes would circulate the bad news, the heroics, and the usual latrine rumors that were so much a part of Army life.

Hap Helder, so named because of his ever-present smile—which was partially caused by his protruding upper teeth—was the man of the hour the second day on Peleliu. He was hailed by an officer who was dressed as a pilot. On picking up the stranger he learned of the flyer's plight.

"Could you get me some one-hundred high-octane gas for my plane?" the pilot asked. "You see, I'm from a carrier and was forced to land here because I'm out of fuel."

Hap rendezvoused with several LSTs before he found one stocked with one-hundred high-octane. A couple of barrels were promptly loaded into the DUKW, and they were off to refuel the plane.

When the entrenched Japanese on the escarpment saw the hustle around the plane, they proceeded to bring it under fire. Like a team, the Marines encircled the airfield, and brought all guns into play to silence the guns on the escarpment.

Seldom, if ever, has a warplane been refueled with helmets carried in fire-brigade fashion from fuel barrel to fuel tank.

"Fill the holes for takeoff," shouted the pilot.

Again, Marines with helmets and trenching shovels carried and scraped coral together to fill the worst of the bomb craters. The gunnery duel between Marines and Japanese became a small-scale war as the dramatics were enacted in real life.

His plane loaded with fuel, the pilot explained to the ground crew that they were to hold back on his wings until he gave them a release signal by holding up his arm, at which time the plane would be revved up enough to make a quick takeoff.

Happily, the plane's engine kicked off on the first start attempt. The pilot literally warmed it up on the first rev of his motor, then gradually picking up thrust, signaled for the men to release his wings. A few bounces down the runway, a few crazy ricochets, and then the corsair shot into the air like a homing pigeon—with a shout of triumph and exultation from the ground crew, who had miraculously sped another hero on his way to join his carrier.

* * *

Loss of the previous night's sleep made weary men of the drivers of those DUKWs that were still operable. Drivers who had lost their DUKWs assisted in whatever way they could as assistant drivers, unloading cargo or helping the maintenance crew work on equipment.

The password given to us that night was hard to pronounce. (Passwords always contained the letter L because Japanese can't pronounce an L distinctly, but neither could a foreign-born chap from New York.)

As the drivers dozed off, their sleep was interrupted by gunfire, flares, and finally a startling, challenging demand, "Give me the password!"

It was repeated; then a shot rang out. We were all on our bellies with our M-1s and carbines cocked ready for firing.

"What the hell happened?" we were asking ourselves. Listening with an attentiveness never exhibited in school, we barely breathed lest we miss a fire order. The tension was broken by an outburst of Yankee swear words. It was a Marine communications officer, giving our officers a dressing down for the shooting of one of his men working on a faulty communication line.

The man with the wounded shoulder was a New Yorker who, when asked, started stuttering the password with a broken dialect. His stuttering had so unnerved our DUKW driver that he pulled the trigger. Our company commander ordered Jess Hinks to evacuate the man to the hospital ship. Hinks later reported the man's injury was well treated and not as bad as first believed.

The men were jittery beyond description. After the shooting they put their rifles aside and drew their bayonets from the scabbards. Under each weary soldier's head lay his unsheathed bayonet, ready for instant use.

It was partially a nightmare that woke Adrian Greg, and with a tremendous flurry of his bayonet he put aside his imaginary Japanese intruder. He had stabbed Hinks in the arm. Hinks brought Greg back to normalcy by cursing him severely. "But I know there was a Japanese hand in my face," complained Greg.

"Japanese hell," said Jess, "it was this damn sand crab." Whereupon he held up a four-inch crab that had crawled under his ammunition belt.

From the crudest form of pioneering we seemed to have reverted back to barbarism, where killing was our only objective in life!

So ended our only overnight stay in this area. It became the island cemetery when the grave's registration detachment came ashore to bury the heroes of Peleliu.

Our camp was moved northward to an area on the airstrip alongside the Japanese torpedo station. Hinks and I, dog-tired, came back to find that the new bivouac area had been assigned. We trudged up to this encampment as darkness settled over the island. We were challenged, but cussed the jackasses in such outspoken English that we were allowed to pass. Life under such pressure was rubbing everyone's nerves to a frazzle.

When we reached our company, the men whose DUKWs had been destroyed during the first two days had their foxholes dug. Tired as we were, we asked for help but got a negative response. Our top sergeant, hearing our downright outlandish bitching and name-calling, came to our rescue.

Said the sergeant, "I had the men dig a hole over near that old frame building for two of our officers. However, I don't think they're coming ashore, but will spend the night on a ship. You can take it."

Hinks and I were speculating as to the size of the ship our officers thought would be safe. "Probably took a battleship," said Hinks.

We were laying out our bedding when we heard twigs snapping in the brush. We froze stiff and got down low in the foxhole. We could still hear the snapping as we held a quick council of war.

"Sure as hell they're Japanese snipers, but what to do?" I whispered. My comrade suggested asking for the password. I did.

The noise of my booming voice was swallowed by the tense silence that precedes the spring of a cat upon its prey. Only the distant rat-tat-tat of machine guns and the thump-thump of our hearts were audible.

Again the crackling noise, and again we got down low in our foxhole and held another council of war. Finally, I agreed to rout the Japanese with the new M-1 Greg had picked up for me on one of his trips to the front lines.

I asked for the password and the noise abruptly stopped. With my patience exhausted and my nerves on edge, I started into the brush, shouting, "Give me the password. Give me the password."

I had nearly reached the spot where the crackling noise was first heard when a sudden burst of flurry froze me to the spot. Two bantam chickens had taken to wing with the damnedest fluttering and squawking ever beaten into a man's brain.

I returned to our foxhole limp and speechless. Hinks needed no encouragement. He picked up our bedding, and we went back to the bivouac area and crowded our bedding into Lard Bell's foxhole. He was still complaining when I fell asleep.

Some say there were three bombs dropped, but I heard only the last one. I was awakened by Bell's foot in my face as he started for the bomb-proof cellar that the Japanese had abandoned when driven from the airstrip back into the hills. His absence from the foxhole gave the rest of us all the room necessary for a comfortable rest!

It was this same night that leaflets were dropped by a Japanese plane, which later was shot down in the ocean, according to a rumor heard the next day. They said, "Honorable Admiral Halsey has suffered much casualty. Nippon Navy supreme, Yankees to be defeated. Strong force from Japan on way to crush enemy. No quarters to be given. Japanese Imperial Army."

On the third night a machine gunner parked himself on the top escarpment above the airstrip. Before the darkness would reveal his gun flashes, he would peel off a Ta-ta-ta, Ta-ta-ta, Ta! Ta-ta-ta, Ta-ta-ta, Ta! His proficiency and smoothness of handling his gun assured those of us dug in on the beaches that one outpost had a master machine gunner on the job!

A DUKW still floats after being hit by a mortar on Peleliu

75

On the fourth night he repeated his soliloquy. Came the fifth night, we were elated to hear his challenging flirtation of "come and get me if you can outgun me." This time it was from a new position, and further in the hill. His nightly reports were a morale booster that is worthy of a long-ago, gratefully acknowledged thanks.

On the fourth day I was hauling ammunition along the airstrip. While waiting for an unloading crew, I decided to leave the DUKW and walk up the strip toward a log, where I planned to eat my lunch. A dead Marine, covered by a poncho, was lying at the end of the log. Saying a prayer and giving grace, I opened my eyes and, while gazing at the ground, observed a coin, which turned out to be a badly discolored 1943 Abe Lincoln penny. Its condition indicated that it had been here for much longer than the four days of combat.

Reflecting on this, I remembered reading that a few 1943 coins had been minted and given to generals and admirals at the beginning of the war for good luck souvenirs. In all probability this coin had been taken from an Allied officer and, in turn, been lost by the captor who had taken it from the officer. On the other hand, some admiral or general could have passed this way while being taken to a prisoner camp, and could have lost it himself prior to D-Day.

The newly found penny became my good luck symbol and was carried in my seashell tool kit. On returning to civilian life it was carried in my wallet. At the grand opening of a discount store in Bellevue, Washington, in 1958, the penny fell out of my wallet, rolled under a counter, and fell through a crack. Some years later I read in a Seattle newspaper that a 1943 copper penny was found by a bank in Bellevue, and the coin was appraised at two thousand dollars. The new owner will be amazed to know how this coin came to the Northwest!

Our next bivouac move, which turned out to be our permanent one until we left the island, was to the northeast end of the airstrip past Bloody Nose Ridge. Behind our camp the Marines had a secondary defense line.

It was at this last site that Bell came running into camp one afternoon to pant and gasp out the announcement that the Japanese ammunition dump had caught fire and was blowing up. His anxiety sobered all who were in camp. Soon we could hear some moderate explosions. Within a half hour the bursts became deafening. Some artillery shells exploded and trailed smoke for a quarter of a mile across the sky. It was a magnificent spectacle, but one that bordered on fear. It was cause for the Air Corps to disperse all planes to the far extremities of the airfield.

With the ever-increasing intensity of the exploding Japanese shells, the remnant of Japanese soldiers entrenched in the caves in the Peleliu hills staged an offensive, only to be driven back—never to realize that the misleading bombardment was only the burning of their ammunition dump.

After fifteen hectic days, the Marines announced to the world that the island was secured. Those of us experiencing combat for the first time wondered at their sanity. It wasn't safe to climb the first escarpment, for I was shot at and missed three times before a Marine shouted, "Get off the skyline unless you want to die." A weak-eyed Japanese soldier had barely missed his target as his bullets went screaming overhead.

Lou McClosky, while hauling freight, witnessed a Marine drop off an alligator as it was plowing over the coral reef. McClosky promptly dove in and rescued the Marine while the alligator continued on its mission, the crew oblivious of what had happened to their gunner. Belts of ammunition would have drowned him had McClosky not gone to the rescue. On our return to Pavuvu, he was awarded the Soldier's Medal.

* * *

After the secured announcement was made, general relaxation of fears and tensions came over the entire fighting force. Engineers had drilled a well, and the restrictions on the use of water were lifted. After fifteen long, sweaty days, we were able to undress, fill our helmets with water, take a bath, and put on clean clothes. It was a great morale builder!

One of the marks on nearly every combatant was chapped lips. Heat was one of the contributing factors, but another was the habit of breathing through the mouth to lessen the noise barrier in tense situations—this would bypass the nose, which gave off sounds.

Dysentery was another combat problem that was best handled by the corpsmen. Loe, our Navy corpsman, would mix a potent drink resembling a peppermint shake, which was soothing to the stomach and would aid in eliminating the intestinal convulsions.

After the island was secured, combat went swirling away into the hills. Some degree of relaxation caught three drivers sitting on a crate when Greg drove up. "You guys should be ashamed for goofing off," he said in a loud, sharp, derogatory voice. "Do you know the Marines up on the hill are fighting the enemy with rocks because they don't have ammunition?"

"Greg, tell us you fell off your DUKW and landed on your head," answered one of the drivers, not a bit responsive to an obvious rumor.

"Battles are fought with bullets, not rocks—if you could only remember!" added another.

"Jeepers, Greg, you've spoiled our whole day," commented the third, without the slightest degree of compassion.

It was months later, while on Okinawa, that we read on the bulletin board that Captain Pope and his company were given a citation for unusual bravery for repulsing the Japanese with rocks, thereby defending their strategic position on Peleliu. Many heroic stories make their rounds, but all too few are deservedly recognized.

Thanksgiving and Christmas were both spent on Peleliu. We were thankful to be alive, and groused little when we were served canned turkey on both occasions. Fresh vegetables had long ago vanished from our menu. Fresh meat was impossible to get in quantities large enough to

A First Division marine wounded on Peleliu Island is lifted aboard an amphibious truck for transfer to a hospital ship in the harbor, to be carried to rear base hospitals for further treatment.

feed the company. Occasionally a loin of pork or a few steaks could be swapped for a war souvenir, providing you could find a boat that was recently provisioned with fresh rations.

Hatcher, a Southerner with a trapper's cunning, was able to bait a trap and capture three wild chickens that had lived through the war. In true pioneer spirit, he built a makeshift pen and tenderly cared for them with food and water. By Christmas he was getting two eggs a day—a most liberal return on the garbage fare he fed his flock.

It so happened one day that a couple of Marines from the front line came walking through the camp. When they spotted the chickens, they asked Hatcher if he had any eggs for sale.

"Yes, five for five dollars," was his reply.

He was promptly paid.

The Marines were down the road a block, when they turned and came back for another offer. "How much for the chickens?" one asked.

"Five dollars apiece," said Hatcher.

A U.S. Navy Catholic Chaplain celebrates Mass on Peleliu Island, using an oxcart as an altar. The crew of the DUKW remained aboard their vehicle in case a hurry call interrupted them during Mass. A Japanese administration building, wrecked during an artillery duel, is in the background.

Again, the Marines counted out three five-dollar bills for the fifteen-dollar total, and Hatcher was out of the poultry business!

Once again our operations reverted to normalcy. Seashells did indeed abound in the Peleliu coral. Having located them, it was an effort to get someone to harvest the large crop. Eventually I got three buddies to go with me, after agreeing to pay three cents a shell for all they gathered. We would slit a sock at the top, run a belt through the slot, and drag it alongside of us, leaving our hands free to pick up coral chunks and to scrape off the clinging seashells like potato bugs on the potato vines in Iowa when I was a kid.

They were amazed to find that they could earn thirty dollars during the changing of a tide. Picking up a thousand shells in three hours was an easy job. The work, however, was in cleaning them.

After burying them in a GI stocking for five days, they would be dug up and washed clean. The smell was overpowering when first dug up. To make the cleaning easy we would dig them up, leave them in the sock, and drop the sock in a pail of water. Out on our DUKW, we would tie a heavy string around the sock and drag it to and from the boats while hauling cargo. After a few trips the shells were clean.

After cleaning, to preserve the luster of the shells, we put them in a rubberized bag (one used for Army toilet articles) and subsequently sprinkled the shells generously with tooth powder. Thirty-five years after the war, my unused shells still have their original luster and beauty.

The supply of South Pacific pins was arriving from New York City in ever-increasing numbers. Lillie was mailing two pins in each letter she wrote, which was daily. When an excess of pins was ready, she would make up a box and send fifty at a time. The price was established at five dollars for a completed pin for those in our company and ten dollars for those in other branches of the service.

It was not uncommon for a DUKW driver to bring a Navy souvenir hunter into camp. After seeing the South Pacific crosses, he would invariably buy ten pins, no doubt planning to resell them aboard the ship.

— Chapter V —

Back to Pavuvu

Arriving by boat from Peleliu, we were taken back to our old area. It was the second day after we arrived, and we felt dejected, fatigued, demoralized, and conscious of being deprived of something. No one seemed to give a damn; no one particularly cared to eat. Besides, there was neither stimulation nor incentive to shave and dress neatly. There was definitely no food worthy of waiting out a chow line.

Late in the afternoon we were assembled for the awarding of medals. Our Lou McClosky of the 454th was to get the Soldier's Medal. It was a solemn presentation, with appropriate words said for those left behind. The touching part was that you felt as though you too should have stayed—that those who did stay somehow needed your presence for a protective shield.

Returning to our tent, I put our feelings into a poem that expressed the sentiment of the newly indoctrinated, seasoned troops we had become.

After the smoke of the battle was cleared,
After we leave the battlefield behind,
After caring for the wounded and burying the dead,
After leaving the enemy subdued and shaken with grief,
We board our ships and sail away ... sail away for rest and relief!
There is a trumpet that blows, and a few are honored,
As solemn words are said; we gape around at others
And realize our buddies are numb from battle,
And that others are gone forever.
There are salutes, as orders are shouted,
For soldiers like you and me,
But deep within our soul lies forever,
A saddened philosophy!

81

It's hard to choke back the tears when you are on the world's greatest fighting team, but somehow you do.

On Pavuvu, we were surprised to find a small contingent of Red Cross workers. These very attractive girls were escorted from their patrolled quarters to their jobs, and back to their area by guards. Aside from a pleasant word or two while they were on the job, their associations with enlisted men ended. Strong resentment built up as officers monopolized their time. Girls have a way of communing with boys, and we were aware of their displeasure regarding this arrangement. Further fraternization was demoralizing; visitations became overly formal and eventually ended.

Work began once again. It was a repetition of our first training session, with the amphibious trucks and amtracs attacking an island, then securing it for the day. Returning to base from the day's combat rehearsal, we had a race the magnitude of an Indianapolis 500! Loaded with Marines who gave vocal encouragement, drivers were challenged into getting back to camp before the showers were crowded.

On our way to secure a Marine 37-mm gunner crew, Ors had to check on each side of our DUKW to see if our fenders would clear a wooden gate. (DUKWs had fenders, the same as boats, to avoid bumping too hard against docks and ships.)

"Only an inch to spare," said Ors, as we slowly eased the DUKW through the small opening, which was used to keep stray cattle from roaming too much of the island.

After the 37-mm gun was hoisted into our DUKW, the crew climbed aboard and we were ready for the wild dash. We were off! Soon we hit the hill; the gate was at its bottom. Looking down that hill, the eyes caught the narrowing of the road, which made clearance of our behemoth vehicle seemingly impossible.

"Haul in the bumpers. Get your legs inside," were the final instructions.

Every Marine obeyed, meanwhile visualizing flying wood, as our vehicle careened toward the apparently blocked road at the foot of the hill. Having safely passed through it earlier with the bumpers down, we were confident that the extra eight-inch clearance gained by bringing the bumpers into the DUKW's compartment allowed us to pass through the gate at sixty miles an hour. Downhill gravity, plus the acceleration, had us moving at a roller-coaster speed. From the gleeful "yippee" and "pour it on" comments, it was apparent that the Marines loved the action. When we rocketed through the gate, a gratified "whew" burst from the riders.

A road clogged with amphibian vehicles preceded us. Taking off through the coconut groves, we made a real combat mission of DUKW driving. Arriving at the beach well ahead of the pack, including those who had followed us, we whistled our very authoritative police whistles. As a vehicle slackened its speed, our DUKW went through the slight break in line and was in the water like an excited Labrador retriever!

This day's driving earned Ors and me probably one of the only compliments the Marines ever paid the Army. After we delivered them at their bivouac area, the officer approached us and said, "We have agreed among ourselves that we would like you as our drivers for the next invasion—can we count on you?"

"Sir, our company commander is the one to see regarding our assignment; it would be an honor to drive you, sir."

Either the Marine officer reconsidered his appraisal of our driving ability, or our commanding officer talked him out of it, as the assignment was never discussed further.

* * *

"Let's go to the target area and pick up seashells," suggested a couple of Marines who wanted something out of the ordinary to do on a hot Sunday afternoon.

After lunch we picked out a life raft and paddled to an off-limits target area island, so called because of its distance and visibility of the shells hitting or splashing in the water around it. The size of a battleship with a beautiful reef around it, it looked like an ideal spot. Pulling up to the reef, we were amazed at the number of sharks who had literally woken up and fought their way to deep water.

"They were in here eating the dead fish from our shelling," observed one of the Marines.

"Look at those seashells," exclaimed the other, as we bottomed out on the coral reef.

Over the side we went, with our GI shoes on to protect our feet, a sock hanging from our belt and only a pair of shorts for clothing. Exploding ammunition had killed the seashells. The marine life in the shells had washed out, so we were picking up choice, cleaned shells. Each of us came home with two stockings full—a thousand seashells per man!

Concentrating on making seashell crosses was consuming much leisure time, in addition to becoming a very lucrative hobby. For a private to send home three hundred dollars a month on a fifty-five-dollar paycheck was out of the ordinary. Mother, being the dearest woman ever, had her feminine intuition working overtime and wrote me a letter, putting her mind at ease, with the admonition, "Stop whatever you're doing because it can't be honest."

Babbit, one of my helpers, had improved the strength of the cross and had added a perfectionist's touch to its making, so that it looked as though it had been made by a professional jeweler. Sales were increasing because they were being shown to more GIs, Marines, and Navy personnel. However, we still charged five dollars to the men in our company and ten dollars to members of all other branches of service.

One day we had the opportunity to buy some larger tiger-eye shells at a terrifically low price. After their purchase we reflected on how we could dispose of them.

While working my way through college, one of my part-time jobs was in a perfumery. Why not pack the larger tiger-eye shells with aromatic sachet powder and cotton? We hurriedly ordered the sachet powder, asking my girlfriend Lillie to send it as quickly as possible. She willingly obliged and sent exactly what we wanted, getting a popular aroma from a well-known cosmetic company.

We promptly made five of our new creations, which were named "The South Pacific Seashell Sachet Sensation." Since it entailed only one shell, and took little time to attach to the South Pacific pin, we decided that seven dollars and fifty cents was a reasonable price—one that any soldier could afford. To our astonishment the new line was an instant success.

Putting eight crosses and two South Pacific Seashell Sachet Sensations in a cigar box, with three inches by five inches of cotton batting for a display pillow under the jewelry, we would hit the various camps on payday.

Coming upon a crap game, I'd open the cigar box and allow the perfume, comparable to a magnolia-scented garden in springtime, to waft out. It reminded the boys about bygone romances.

"Give me three," the big winner would order.

Moving down the line of crap and poker games, we would get a similar order from each winner. Returning an hour later, the first game would have another winner, who in turn ordered one or two.

During the interim of my first showing and my return, the perfume had time to reach those invisible GIs taking a break on their bunks, who recoiled from their semiconsciousness, shouting, "Girls in camp!"—only to find an irresistible piece of jewelry exuding a sensuous aroma!

By the time we left Pavuvu for our invasion on Okinawa, monthly sales had soared to five hundred dollars. Salesmanship took a while to cultivate, but with a good product your confidence mounts!

— Chapter VI —

Off to Okinawa

Pavuvu was a training period of short duration, with a feeling growing within each of us that we had been lucky on our first invasion.

As before, all our worldly possessions were put in our barracks bags. Some carried a foot locker for extras. These extras could include war clubs from Guadalcanal, rifles from Peleliu, or tools and supplies to continue hobbies should time permit. Stashed away for our continued comfort were the mattresses issued by the Navy. Rear hatches of our DUKWs were loaded without personal necessities. Strapped to the steering column of DUKW 417 was my gas mask, which I had vowed never again to be caught without.

On our gun mounts, behind the driver's seat, fifty-caliber machine guns were mounted. We were to have extra firepower for Okinawa.

We were briefed on what to expect and how to cope with obstacles. We were cautioned not to eat Okinawan food because of night soil, contamination, and deliberate poisoning. Civilians were expected, but under no circumstances was there to be fraternization, as sixty-five percent of the women had venereal disease.

Venomous snakes were known to be on the island, so we were instructed on how to treat snakebite wounds. We all received booster shots and were read the articles of war—reminding us that striking an officer was as bad as facing the enemy without a gun. Finally, under international code, if captured, all we were to give the enemy was our name, rank, and serial number. Our common concern was whether the enemy understood, or for that matter, cared!

We all received our assignments, were loaded on various boats, and put to sea on a venture that was to be the invasion of Okinawa.

Seasoned troops had even less to say. They didn't even ask a question, knowing that the answer was already implanted in their minds: to kill before getting killed.

Our DUKW was hoisted by the ship's winch and set down on a landing barge, which was already twenty feet above the ship's deck. We were twenty-six feet in the air when we were sitting in the driver's seat!

Alex Kar, the driver-in-charge, decided to sleep on our DUKW topside, where we could watch the stars and enjoy the cool evening breeze, if there was any.

Again we were wearing impregnated coveralls, making us feel uncomfortably warm, since nobody wore anything but trousers and cap while off duty on Pavuvu. Our arrangement was working perfectly; in fact it was ideal—privacy, refreshing breezes, and the heavenly display of a bedspread of stars that winked at you from a flirtatious, romantic sundown until daybreak.

A heavy sea started one afternoon, causing the boat to roll. As the wind picked up velocity, the boat pitched and rolled with increased vigor. By the time we finished chow and came on deck, the wind was commanding attention by literally whistling through the rigging. Lurching and pitching soon shook the supper from those inclined to suffer from seasickness. At times our boat would settle in a trough, making it impossible to see any of the other ships.

Kar and I worked our way over the boat deck, up the rigging, to the landing barge, where we covered our DUKW with a tarpaulin to keep off any salt spray. Settling down for the night, we would fix on a star, then watch it disappear as the ship would roll to starboard. Slowly the ship would right itself, only to continue the roll to port, with the star disappearing on the opposite side.

After commenting on this phenomenon several times, Kar turned his attention to the rigging holding the landing barge in place. Next to come under his scrutiny were the small cables that anchored our DUKW on the barge.

"Ya know, this is getting to be one hell of a wind, and if any one of these cables snapped we'd never be heard of again," said a concerned Kar.

"Maybe we're to be spared from a worse death should we make the invasion," I replied.

"Nuts," responded Kar. "I've got to go to the head."

"Over the side," I suggested, "but not into the wind." Idle words, as Kar was already slithering ever so carefully down the rigging on the way to the head.

Blackness slowly swallowed the whole convoy, as stars were obliterated and a few splatterings of rain beat down on the tarpaulin. Men grow concerned about each other if their appearance at a given time is overly delayed. Enough time had elapsed for Kar to have gone through a complete toilet, including a shower!

Could he have slipped and gone overboard? Could he have hurt himself going down the hatch? Each delayed minute created a greater tragedy, until I could picture him dead from having slipped and fallen, due partially to my delay in rushing to his rescue.

It was my turn to slither down the rigging, and the hardship dictated that returning would be pure folly. I, too, would stay below deck. Through the blackout curtains, down the lighted hatch, and into the head I proceeded, wondering if he could be found. Hopefully, he could be suffering from only a mild case of seasickness.

Walking into the head caused a gastronomical upheaval that would years later induce sympathetic upchucking reflexes upon the slightest association with any one of the myriad sights now before my eyes. On the floor was six inches of water, sloshing from side to side as the ship rolled. Latrines had not been flushed, and had cast their waste from the bowl. Urinals had slopped over, adding to the stench; cigarette butts floated around like lost corks from bottles of sulfuric odors.

"Alex, let's get out of here," I suggested.

"I'm staying," said Kar. "I can't stand that height."

I left the eight seasick GIs and Kar to their fate, as they stood on the benches to keep out of the sloshing water.

As I climbed up the rigging, a few deep breaths eased the pain in my lungs from the ordeal I had gone through. It was a trying night with news that we had skirted a typhoon.

It seemed as though the convoy was growing. Occasionally a battle wagon or an aircraft carrier could be seen on the horizon. Several times torpedo boats raced through the convoy. We witnessed the dropping of depth charges, but no flotsam came to the surface.

Gunnery practice for the ships was a diversion. A plane, with a trailing target, would fly by the ship gunners trying to hit the target. Picture the consternation of the pilot when the gunners shot the tow rope in two, just behind the plane!

Because of the secrecy, the prohibition on keeping a diary, and the ban of all photography, the date, historic facts, and the precise words spoken on our stop at Mogmog on Ulithi Island will be lost forever, except for the retelling of this drinking party.

This hilarious experience began when word was passed that all combatants would go ashore for a beer bust on Mogmog. On our boat were several DUKW drivers who had developed a great liking for parties, having been deprived of this pleasure some seventeen months. Drinking beer that was actually legal instead of being stolen was, in itself, a step in the right direction. For once we needn't worry about being on the wrong side of the law.

A boat was sent alongside of our ship, and among those going ashore were four of our stalwart drivers, who never realized the commotion these Army souls could create on this Navy stronghold.

Stach, with his cap bill pushed up like an officer's, said he would be in charge of getting our allotment of beer—which was to be six bottles apiece. When he stepped up to the window he said to the sergeant distributing the beer, "Give my men four cases for my company."

Since there were four men, we all carried a case. Obviously the dispensing sergeant thought Stach was an officer, because all officers wore their pins under their cap bills and under their shoulder straps so that they couldn't be identified, except close up.

Stach's ruse had worked, and the four of us sat down to a drinking party. Our guest turned out to be a red-headed Irishman who, seeing us with a quantity of beer, asked if he might have a bottle.

"Only if you'll sing us a song," ordered Stach.

The Irishman promptly gave us a rendition of "McNamara's Band." His bottle empty, he offered to repeat the song for a second one. Well, the singing went on and so did the drinking. Perhaps the singer's voice paled as the day wore on, but our spirits kept soaring. We would join in the chorus. Spectators crowded around just to do the boom-boom-boom-booms for "McNamara's Band." Just to stand up after the drinking party was something of an effort.

The order to load ship was given and we slowly started our trek toward the boat. Unfortunately, the Marine officer was coming from the opposite direction and either he or Stach staggered at the wrong time. There was body contact. The officer slapped Stach's bill down to see if he was wearing bars; no bars! Stach, with a pugnacious attitude, took this to signify a swing of a fist, and released two haymakers that fell far short of their mark.

"A fight," someone on the boat shouted.

All the enlisted men jumped ashore to witness a real beer-barrel brawl. Officers, who had boarded their launch, likewise returned to stop whatever was going amiss. In the shore patrol tower, a clangor sounded, and the area swarmed with law enforcement.

No blows landed, but four Army DUKW drivers, attached to the Marines for combat, spent the night in the brig to sober up. The next day, before sailing, we returned to our ship, where extra duty was assigned. This duty entailed supplying the kitchen with certain items from the ship's hold. Cases of Coca-Cola started coming through the chain gang line. We alerted other drivers, who were thrown every fifth case, thereby assuring us of our supply of Coke for the remainder of the trip.

— Chapter VII —

Okinawa Landing

April 1, 1945, was D-Day. This was both April Fool's Day and Easter Sunday. We were unloaded and were rendezvousing, waiting for our signal to dispatch to the beach.

An observation plane, launched from a battleship, came flying over the convoy. Some gunner aboard ship started shooting. Tracers indicated the target was not being hit. However, the pilot, who was very conscious that he was being fired at, immediately put his plane in a steep bank so that the stars on his wings were plainly visible. The shooting stopped; the pilot continued his mission.

The Marines were to land on Purple Beach, and given eleven days to secure their objective, which was the capture of Yontan Airstrip (called Yomitan by the Japanese). By the time our eleventh wave came ashore with reinforcements, the word was already back that the airstrip was secured. It was done without opposition. Amtracs and DUKWs worked throughout the day without interference.

In the afternoon, a cave was discovered near the beach with countless suitcases and trunks of clothing. About dusk, someone shouted, "Enemy planes!" Unconcerned, we stopped to watch these two small planes slowly fly over our area, then out to the gigantic armada off the shore. When the ships opened up with their antiaircraft guns it looked like a thousand blackbirds pecking away at an eagle. It apparently was the intention of the flyers to crash their planes into one of our ships. However, they crashed short of their goals. We had witnessed our first kamikaze attack.

After the kamikaze planes were wiped out, we were back on the island exploring every conceivable nook and cranny. A few shots were heard but there were no bursts of fire that would indicate a strong defense.

The cave containing trunks and clothes was relocated. A large tree trunk, with cleats serving as a ladder, stood at the entrance. A guard was posted, making it off limits to those of us who had been there before. Nevertheless, an overpowering desire to actually see what these natives looked like caused me to do some fast thinking. Soon I had my chance. A sergeant came up the ladder and asked the guard if the interpreter had arrived.

"Haven't seen him, sergeant," replied the guard, whereupon the sergeant went below.

Calling to Tom Haze, one of our drivers, a handsome dude with a college look about him, I said, "Follow me, you're an interpreter."

Coming up to the guard, I introduced him to Tom Haze, interpreter. "They are looking for you," said the guard.

Tom was as intrigued as I at the sight of men, women, and children. They were talking Japanese in various tones and decibels. Women were

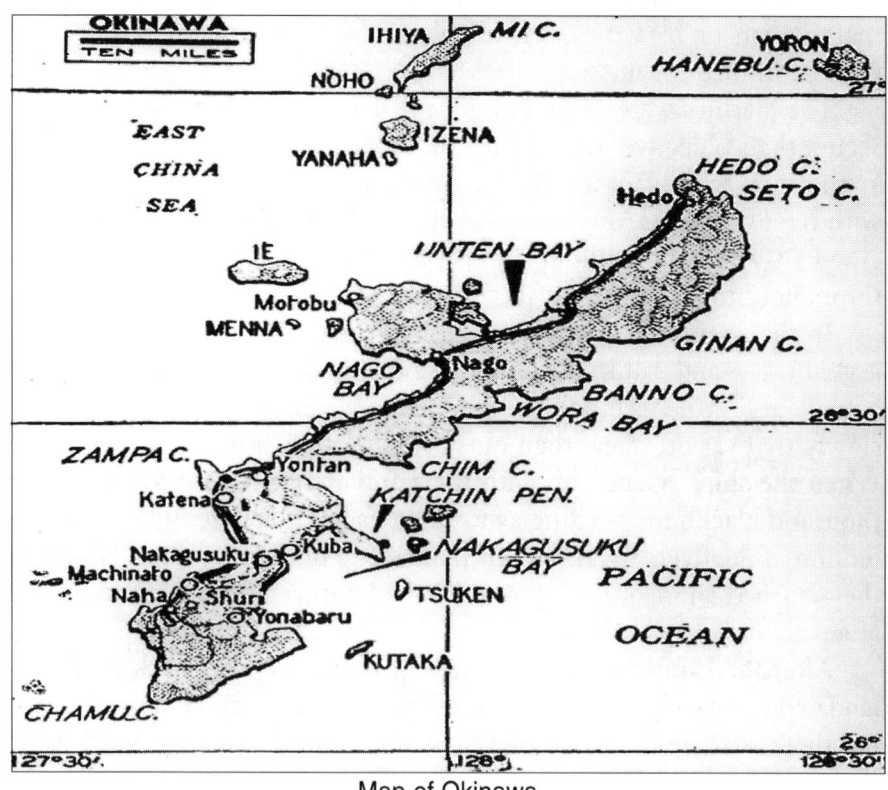

Map of Okinawa

trying to unscramble the mess of clothes, household possessions, and personal effects. For the most part the men were sitting down. (These were tired-looking old men with deep lines in their faces.) A large hole, which you could enter by stooping, was on the uphill side of the cave. A Marine guard was already stationed there to see that no one passed, or that no enemy soldiers escaped.

It was growing dark in the cave but lights had been hooked up—power being made by a small generator which was running topside at the entrance of the cave. This was war, but the first care of these Marines was the welfare of the civilians. It made one proud to be fighting with them.

Sitting on a rock on the uphill side of the cave within speaking distance of the guard, I was reflecting on the day's fortunate circumstances when an old man approached. I returned his bow with a nod of my head; he sat down, smiled, and then said a few words in Japanese. His smile, interpreted as a sign of friendship, was more to my liking than a clenched fist.

Before I realized it, I started chewing on a piece of chocolate he had offered me. Remembering the preinvasion lectures, I promptly started spitting it out, rinsing my mouth with my canteen of water. I gave him a

Assault troops of U.S. Task Force landing on beach of Okinawa in the Ryukyus.

packet of C-rations, then looked up my interpreter, Tom, and we left the place. As long as I was on the island, I never visited the place again. Undoubtedly this cave had served the natives well when their homeland had been bombed and shelled.

One DUKW, coming ashore on D-Day, was wedged in a coral island crevice and couldn't free itself. When the tide went out, it was high and dry. However, when the tide came in, the DUKW as well as the island was completely submerged. After several days the DUKW was removed and used for parts.

Around dusk, the ships at anchor started their fog machines, blanketing the area with a heavy fog. Nothing at sea was visible to those of us on the beach. As the evening wore on, the fog drifted over the beach and island, making the area a very difficult bombing target. All night the fog was dispensed, but it didn't discourage the enemy.

About 11 P.M. an air raid alarm was sounded. An enemy plane came in, dropping several bombs, and made a direct hit on a DUKW belonging to another company. Gasoline and tires made a spectacular fire, but no effort was made to put it out. Men stayed in their foxholes. There was some speculation that the plane would never make it back to Japan.

When morning arrived, we prepared a small fire, made coffee, and ate our C-rations. It was not the breakfast that was gratifying; it was the shared feeling of relief that this operation wasn't as devastating as Peleliu. We liked the idea of a fire because the Okinawan northern latitude was chilling, compared to the tropical climate we had left behind at the equator. We cooked and kidded each other about being the world's worst soldiers. The meal proved to be a break that released many tensions.

Single shots heard the first day were finally explained, but were priority secrets among those who participated. Each house had a stone wall and hedge around it. This wall was a retainer fence for the family hog. Marines, craving a taste of fresh meat and having so easily accomplished their mission by securing Yontan Air Base in a matter of hours, had returned to butcher the family hogs. This was done with such expertise that the smell of frying pork chops wafted through the spring air on our second day on Okinawa.

On hearing that my buddies had turned into butchers, there was but one thing to do—remind them of our preinvasion orders to eat nothing because it might be contaminated.

"Dummy," explained the man holding the frying pan. "You don't have to eat it, but what the hell do you suppose the natives do with these hogs?" Not waiting for an answer, he added, "They eat 'em like we're going to do!"

No pork chops ever tasted better!

* * *

April 3 was a cold, rainy day, encouraging the use of our field jackets. For some reason, a group of natives had emerged from their hiding place and had gathered at our operation area.

Bewildered, hungry, unable to communicate with their captors, and leading children crying from fear, they were a sorrowful sight. In shamed modesty, one wrinkled old man—toothless, skin and bones—kept in a crouched position to hide his private organs. Greg, seeing the misery of the old man, removed his field jacket and helped the man put it on. (Greg's generosity was boundless and his heart was as big as the great Pacific.)

There was a lifting of the man's heavy furrowed brow. He pulled himself together and, when he reached his full height, he crossed his chest with one arm and saluted Greg with a graceful, humble bow that made it a pleasure giving away a field jacket. No doubt, if the old man didn't die from pneumonia after his exposure, he passed this touching story, this act of humanity, on to his children, grandchildren, and God willing, his great-grandchildren. An act of kindness in this new world was as rewarding as any act of kindness told in the Bible.

On delivering cargo up front the following day, we drove through beautiful country with rolling hills, coming to rest in the gardens the natives were cultivating. All land was neatly terraced and every level plat of ground was planted. On our return trip our eyes scanned the area and reveled in its serenity, the beauty of the landscape, and the meticulous work the natives had done to create a veritable picture that excited the seven senses of man.

Ahead of us was a parked DUKW.

"Stop and see what's wrong," shouted Ors.

We weren't completely stopped when a driver came running toward us as if an enraged animal, the size of a Brahma bull was only a jump behind.

"Get out of here," he screamed. "There's Japanese in a tunnel under that hill."

95

Mounting his DUKW, he drove off as if he had business elsewhere.

"Let's check it out, Steve. Surely if there were soldiers in that tunnel that driver would never have lived to tell us."

"OK, I'll stand by," replied Steve.

As I approached the tunnel I could hear voices; a child was crying. Speaking so as to let them know I was approaching, I concluded it must be a family. Getting on my hands and knees I peered into the cave, knowing I was facing humans, not cavemen or dinosaurs. Their voices became excitable but were utterly unintelligible. Slowly my eyes distinguished various cooking utensils, dishes, a teapot, and a few vegetables. Now I could see faces of both women and children. Try as I might, I could not get them to follow me from what they regarded as their castle. They had water, food, and comparative safety in this cave, and were not about to leave.

After insisting, with no results, I decided to take their teakettle with me, depriving them of one of life's necessities. A murmur of protest came from the women, with one stretching out her hand. From her imploring tone it was obvious she wanted the teakettle very badly. After all, I was only trying to coax them out—what the hell, let her keep the teakettle. So, I handed it back.

She nodded her head, a gesture of thanks, and passed it to the woman next to her. Lifting the kettle, she drank heartily from the spout, passing it on to the next woman. After the women and the children had each had a drink, it was returned to the one who had taken it from me. After she drank, it was handed back to me—empty.

They had dispensed their supply of drinking water, and no doubt dreaded the thought of trying to get more, with the likelihood of being shot foremost on their mind. Disgusted with myself for not being able to convince them that I was a friend, I left the teakettle and slowly backed out of the cave.

In the distance were a couple of other GIs walking around unarmed, so I shouted, "We need an interpreter."

They walked over to where I was, and the first thing they asked was, "Have you seen any Okinawans?"

"There's a tunnel full of them," I said, pointing to the hole at the foot of the hill.

"We're here to get them to go to the compound," said the taller of the two. "Ned is an interpreter and will have a talk with them."

His Japanese apparently was more persuasive than my acts of kindness, as he crawled out of the cave with fourteen women and children following him.

We helped them on our DUKW and, with the interpreter and his buddy, started for the compound. On the way, a can of salmon stashed away on our DUKW was opened and the contents were offered to the children. They no doubt had been indoctrinated too, for they refused to even taste the delicacy offered to them!

Our reward was to come when the natives were unloaded at the compound. Faces, previously reflecting only fear and mistrust, for the first time registered hope. They recognized cleanly dressed, smiling friends and neighbors, who greeted them in Japanese and who may have said, "God bless those who have delivered you!"

* * *

With astonishing rapidity the engineers put bulldozers, road graders, and rock crushers to work building roads. The narrow paths on Okinawa were meant for wagon and horse; our equipment needed roads five times as wide. Each day these roads were extended. So fast was the change that we often took drivers around just to see the magnificent job done by the engineer battalions on the island—both Marines and Seabees.

There were three Marine divisions and the Tenth Army to mold the island into a modern highway system, which they did with vigor. Their colossal achievements only spurred them to greater goals.

Our camp was set up on a hillside just below the west end of Yontan Airstrip. Unfortunately for us, the airstrip was to prove a target for later Japanese bombings. However, from the altitude they were dropped, the bombs carried over the end of the strip and into our camp.

Below us about 300 yards was a coral pit where coral rock was blasted loose, crushed, and made into aggregate for roads. Eight hundred yards below us was the beach. Our view of the East China Sea was beautiful, and the immense fleet at anchor was assurance enough that Uncle Sam had come to stay!

We all pitched tents, then dug foxholes big enough to accommodate six men. Sacks of sand were piled four high around the dugout hole. The entrance was open with a protective pile of sandbags on each side of it.

Invasion ships stand off the island of Okinawa, Ryukyu Islands, on D Plus Two Day. In the left center of the photo is the airfield of Yontan which fell to the American troops on the first day of the invasion. Aerial view.

The dirt from the hole was then thrown up against the sandbags. The foxhole would then be four feet high with a tapered wall on the outside, starting at the bottom as five feet and tapering out at the top at two feet. Boards were put on top, with some men going as far as to cover the boards with dirt. A tarpaulin over this would reduce the chances of getting wet, so all of us weatherized our second home.

It became routine for the ships to cover themselves for the night by starting fog machinery, burning diesel fuel, and creating steam. This smokescreen was very effective and, since the majority of supplies were stocked only a short distance from the shoreline, they too were protected. Several fog machines were also located on the beach for effectiveness.

Also routine was the air raid alert about 11 P.M. every night. This was so customary that there were those who swore they could hear the click of the switch that started the siren.

It was the first night on shore for the company staff. Joe Hulz, who wore a handlebar mustache and who was rated a cook although he was a genius as a photographer, walked around camp, getting oriented.

"You better be ready for the air raid, Joe," cautioned one of his tent mates.

"You don't get bombed, do you?" questioned Hulz.

"No, but we do have air raids, and we do get into our foxholes, just in case," replied Hulz's buddy.

Hulz, thinking he was being spoofed, treated the warning lightly. He went to bed, mindfully folding his clothes neatly and placing them under the head of his bed. After a restless hour, Hulz discovered his problem—his head was lower than his feet! He then reversed his position.

Routinely at 11 P.M. the aircraft warning sounded. Hulz was not only amazed, he was frightened. He reached under what was not the head of the bed to grab his clothes. Having forgotten to move his clothes earlier when he had reversed his position, Joe arrived at the foxhole befuddled, panicked, and bereft of clothes!

* * *

One night, arriving at camp from a late driving assignment, I missed the evening meal at the mess hall. Good-heartedly, Babbit volunteered to do something about it. He then proceeded to fix a quick, satisfying, nourishing meal from a few leftovers. Mutton, a Virginia buddy, decided to visit with me while dinner was being prepared.

"I'll have a coffee, Babbit," he said.

"Coffee coming up."

There we sat—Mutton sipping coffee, while I was trying to make the most of Babbit's offering. Babbit, meanwhile, was waiting for either a thank you or a compliment.

"Hurry, finish eating, it's getting toward air raid time," cautioned Mutton.

"Let me relish Babbit's leftovers," I replied.

However, Mutton's anxiety was growing as my dinner all too slowly disappeared. Again he reminded me of the pending deadline, following this statement by raising his cup toward his mouth for a sip of hot coffee.

At that precise moment, an unusually heavy charge of blasting powder was detonated in the rock quarry. Mutton's nerves were set to be triggered. With the quarry blast, Mutton's arm flexed upward, dashing the cup of hot coffee in his face. Without wiping his face, he jumped to his feet and said, "I'm heading for my foxhole."

Had Babbit not joined us, nobody would have been around to witness the only coffee casualty in our company.

There comes a time in a man's life when he grows so tired and weary that he will actually gamble with his life. How many nights at 11 P.M. had we heard the switch click and jumped into our foxhole before the siren started wailing?

It had been a tiring day, and the light catnaps weren't doing anything for my worn-out body. Defying the air raid alarm, I lay on my bunk, thinking first that the plane would never make it, second that it would drop its bombs elsewhere, and third that the antiaircraft gunners on the island would bag him. Such thinking also kept me awake. Cocking my ear, I tuned in on the peculiar hum a Japanese World War II plane always made. There was one over the island all right, but the hum seemed very far away and I was extremely tired. This was the only accurate reasoning I did all night. Far away meant the plane was coming in unusually high.

At times I nearly chickened out and headed for the hole, but since nothing happened nor was anything happening, I felt as secure as a rabbit must feel hiding in a corn shock with hunters stalking all over the field. No antiaircraft sounded, no tracking lights flashed, and no warning was shouted by the sentry, yet balls of fire and explosion were all over the place.

One jump and I was in the foxhole, hitting a rock so hard with my knee, I thought my leg had been hit by shrapnel.

"What's happening?" asked my buddies who had heeded the siren's warning.

My bruised knee was so shockingly painful I couldn't answer. When my speech returned, after the pain and the paralyzing fear had left, I answered, "We've been bombed."

"Don't you think we have ears? Anybody hurt?" came a reply.

"Don't know. I just saw four balls of fire as big as a jeep."

We listened and tracked the plane until its northern journey was out of hearing range; then we all emerged from our holes to assess the damage.

A new experience presented itself. No one was killed, only one man was moaning.

"Who is it?" I asked.

"Millen's been hit!" came the reply.

Millen was another doubting Tom who believed that bombs were meant for the other guy. He was rushed to the hospital ship, where the metal from the antipersonnel bomb was removed.

Coming in at an angle, the bomb had exploded under Millen's bunk. Had it been a foot higher…we all felt a chill! Looking over Millen's bunk, we noticed that the canvas webbing was torn as if a lion had slashed it with its claws; the bottom mattress was chewed up into fragments and the second mattress, on which Millen slept, had holes through it where the metal entered Millen's back. The two mattresses saved his life. It had paid Millen to sleep in comfort!

From Millen's bloody mattress, Stach went to his cot, jerked back the blanket, and hopped into the bed. A strange feeling under the mattress, resembling a stick of wood, roused his suspicion that he was in bed with a bomb. Slowly rolling out of bed, he picked up the upper half of his mattress, and there lay the bomb. It had nicked the front cleat of his cot, and deflected itself under the mattress. It was intact—two and a half feet long and about three inches in diameter, filled with explosives and metal meant to tear up and demoralize troops. As a demolition expert said, "It's called an antipersonnel bomb."

After a short rest, Millen was returned to our company and assigned to light duty.

Several near misses caused eardrum damage to some of the men. Another, and even more serious injury, was an eye burn from the flashes.

It was 2 A.M. before the camp returned to normalcy, and the grim quiet of slumber crept over weary bodies. Each man was mentally assessing his blessing with closed eyes, but attentive ears turned to the unusual noises that warned of impending danger.

In the still of the night, fifty yards from our foxholes, came the lamenting voice of Boverich: "Why, that bastardly plane bombed both cans of raisin jack that were now ready for drinking!"

Within the week, while on sentry duty, a low-flying enemy plane came in between 11 P.M. and 11:30 P.M. His motors were humming so peculiarly with that individualistic noise that we instantly gave the alarm that an enemy plane was approaching.

Searchlights from the ships penciled through the darkness, trying to get a fix on the plane. No luck. Antiaircraft batteries on the island added their lights to the probe. No luck.

When a low-flying plane dropped its load of phosphorous bombs again in our area, I could see its ghastly outline as it made a forty-five-degree turn, and flew in a southerly direction toward Naha. A small light shone from the bomb bay in the bottom of the plane, and gave away its location only to our camp.

Seconds later it was gone, as the bomb bays closed and the lone marauder miraculously flew away—miraculously because there were hundreds of searchlights from the ships and the ground-based batteries probing the sky. Not one found the plane—all the lights were probing too high. This bomber pilot was not only acquainted with the terrain, but was also very crafty.

In camp, the scattered phosphorous jelly was madly burning, making the whole camp appear as if it was on fire. To those spectators on board ships in the East China Sea, our hillside area must have looked like a forest fire. Not knowing what was to follow, our natural instinct was to extinguish the fire so that our area wasn't illuminated for additional bombs. Everyone started stomping on the burning, jellylike pellets. Twenty minutes of frenzied stomping returned our camp to total darkness.

Loading DUKWs with ammunition from LST 830 at Orange Beach Two on Okinawa in Ryukyus.

Back in the sentry's foxhole, I began asking myself, "Why didn't you shoot down that plane when you saw the light in the bomb bay?" It had been my one chance to have a Japanese flag painted on my DUKW for shooting down an enemy plane, and I had missed my opportunity! Elk, deer, pheasant, and duck hunters have probably faced similar experiences, even during daylight hours—they call it buck fever.

Next morning we were surveying the damage: torn tents, holes burned in tents, and then the climax—our officers' tent was directly hit with the officers in it, causing a total loss, as everything not blown to bits had been consumed by fire. Ingenuity in digging a well-sandbagged foxhole inside the tent had saved their lives. Ironically, a deck of playing cards had been scattered and partially burned. However, lying face up, on top of the sandbags, was the ace of hearts! Our officers no doubt held that card in high esteem for the rest of their lives as an omen of good luck!

Another challenge and confrontation followed two nights later after we had bounced to our foxholes on the first wail of the air raid siren. It was an early 11 P.M. alarm but all hell broke loose on the Yontan Airstrip, just above us, as tracers came screaming over our area. Several explo-

DUKW crossing Bailey Bridge over Asato Gawa River, Okinawa, Ryukyu Islands.

sions followed with flames, shooting hundreds of feet into the air, making the faces of our buddies look a fiery red.

"Must be a war going on," explained Prop.

Within a half hour a sergeant, assisted by an ammunition carrier, quietly issued everyone additional ammunition, sharply ordering every foxhole to keep a guard posted throughout the night. The Japanese had landed several planeloads of commandos and some might have escaped. No commandos ever made it into our area. However, they destroyed several planes and fuel tanks before they were killed.

It was while we were camped on the end of Yontan Airstrip that the first contact with anyone from my home town of Fall City was made. Glen Hamerly, a Seabee who was working a ship that our DUKWs were unloading, asked a driver if he knew my whereabouts. The driver brought him directly to camp as if Hamerly was a VIP entitled to taxi service.

This visit began a succession of contacts with various men from my hometown, each meeting deserving its own celebration and party: Seaman Sid Bates, Lieutenant Commander Tom Mus, Airman Ray Drake, and Infantryman Lyle Bracken, who in 1953–54 was Commander of the Veterans of Foreign Wars Rainier Valley Post, number 2289, in Washington state.

It was a happy day when we were ordered to break camp and to move to a new location. It turned out to be situated on the first road on the right-hand side after the traffic circle heading toward Naha. Ironically, after being through two invasions, the name Easy Street, given to the road, was very popular.

We were back on a twelve-hour day-and-night shift, with supplies coming ashore in unprecedented tonnage figures. We were building Okinawa to be the next bastion for the invasion of Japan.

— Chapter VIII —

Mail Call

Incoming mail was announced with a loud "Mail call!" This endearing sound was given by the company mail clerk whenever he could pick up mail for our outfit. Our Army post office number would change as our various movements to a forward area changed.

Army personnel in the San Francisco area would dispatch mail to us by the quickest means available. Miracles happened! Sometimes it arrived daily, other times weekly; many times it arrived biweekly. A handwritten letter always had the most personality, and was read and reread.

Then the V-mail was opened. It was a sheet of photographed paper that had no warmth, and generally no news, since it was never trusted as being confidential mail—prying eyes could read love secrets meant for two people.

A few local newspapers from home, a magazine, and perhaps an occasional package would arrive. A delayed Christmas package could arrive as much as three months later. Such packages would show the wear and tear of exceptionally long journeys, and often would have one APO crossed off and a new one added, indicating it had made a round trip from San Francisco to a forward area, returned to San Francisco, and then forwarded again. The cookies would be crumbs, worms would be in the nuts, and at one time a salami was discarded to the waste box because the casing was green with mold!

"How come you threw away a salami?" asked Hink when we reported on the contents of our last package from home.

"It was rotten," I assured him.

"Never heard of salami rotting. Let's cut it in two," he optimistically answered.

We did so and the contents looked as good and as appetizing as though they were fresh from the butcher shop. By slicing it thin and serving it with plain bread, it outlasted a case of beer.

Buddies would share news from home and if you didn't volunteer some confidential crumbs of romance from your letter, you were asked, "Doesn't your girlfriend love you any more?"

Once you had completely won the respect of your buddy, you were looked upon as being worthy of the very best, and for the number one rating he would give you his sister's address. He would be confident in his appraisal that you would make a good husband for her, and a welcome brother-in-law.

One package from Tennessee contained a loaf of French bread, with the white of the bread removed, and a pint of whiskey substituted. The crust served as a protective cover for the bottle, which arrived safely, as all good medicine should!

Incoming mail brought news of rifts in the domestic lives of some of the married men. One man, who had left home sixteen months before, received word that his wife was pregnant and that she felt that he would probably want a divorce because of her unfaithfulness. However, he reassured her of his love. The continued correspondence revealed that she was more enthralled by her new lover, and wanted her marriage terminated. It became a problem for the chaplain—a man of wisdom and solace. At least our jilted buddy had someone who would listen to his problem.

Dennis had his own problem. Drafted at the height of a childhood sweetheart romance, his torch was burning bright and hot. In no way was he concerned, interested, or even faintly conscious that other girls existed. His passionate, consuming, heartwarming romance turned drinking aside as an evil which would discredit him in the eyes of his nurse. Cleanliness was a spit-and-polish ordeal with Dennis. It is said he even stood in front of her picture after dressing to get her solemn nod of approval for his deportment.

He brushed his teeth after every meal, as if he were expecting his nurse to walk out of one of her letters, throw her arms around him, and give him an earthshaking French kiss. Dennis was probably the only man in the company who manicured his nails daily—spending that time which other men devoted to playing cards, smoking, shooting dice, or pursuing hobbies.

His bad news couldn't have come through a Dear John letter because it was a blow dealt unkindly by the God of Love—Cupid's blow meant death to his love affair. Dennis ended his displays of propriety and flawless mannerisms; he started drinking, smoking, ignoring his tidy habits, and using profanity as if he had to cast from his body the vile and contemptuous spirits that lurked within his being. His nurse had found and was marrying a new lover. So much bad news in one letter so greatly changed Dennis's habits that the company drunk once asked, when Dennis was observed climbing off his DUKW while under the effects of alcohol, "Do I look and act as crazy as Dennis when I'm drunk?"

"Buddy, you look and act even crazier because you are an old drunk, with lots of practice," was my reply.

"I'm through drinking," he solemnly announced.

Dennis's loss was Dale's gain, for Dale actually quit drinking and came back to the States a sobered man.

Only one man in our company received no mail, and it was a long time before anyone came to understand his problem. He was a likeable fellow and it seemed strange that no one, not even his family, would correspond with him. His pride kept him from admitting that he couldn't write to let anyone know where he was. Once this touching admission was over, his tent mates were helping him catch up with his letters to his family and to his girlfriends.

Through letters came the trickle of news from the States. We saw no daily newspapers and no magazines. There was no radio except for Tokyo Rose, who entertained with sweet music only to ask at the end of the record, "Who's loving your girlfriend back in the States tonight?"

She was constantly babbling propaganda to undermine our morale. This negative approach had the combatants of the Pacific Theatre united on one course of action—to capture her and have her find entertainers for all the uniformed men!

For a while there was a void in communications, which was to be eventually filled when a radio station manned by GIs was set up on Okinawa.

Outgoing mail written by a GI was handled free of charge if it was ordinary mail. Otherwise, it cost six cents if it was to travel by air. It was quickly discovered that all mail was flown by plane. Naturally, we got a free ride, and discontinued buying stamps, which stuck together because of dampness.

Censorship was always a problem because words were cut out of the letter, making the contents confusing and misinforming. All this was for our own good, at least that is what we were told. The enemy intelligence could not learn of our location, or our living conditions, if our mail was properly censored. Our company had one standard; the Marine division had another—they could write anything they wanted to say. There was no censorship. Diaries were collected before leaving for Pavuvu and were supposedly to be sent home, but many never got to the States.

Every Sunday it was my faithful duty to report the week's activities to my parents, with a letter every third day if we were in a forward area. This helped to relieve the worries and frustrations that are every mother's burden when her son is away from home.

Girlfriends would have an answer to their letters as fast as we could whip a few hot thoughts into a passionate, sexual frenzy. At times, life seemed little more than a flicker of light, and every lover wanted that flicker fanned into a passionate, burning blaze!

Girlfriends were our life line for continuing our dreams and our family tree—they were put on pedestals. Also, they could read between the lines to discover that more was expected of them than hugs and kisses. They loved our exploratory probes, and filled their return letters with such promises and more! World War II produced more brides care of the postmaster than any other government agency ever would have believed.

It was on Okinawa that several men in our company came back to me with seashell pins they had purchased, saying they couldn't send them home. Further questioning indicated that Lieutenant Lantern Jaw decided the pin was giving away our position, and therefore was not admissible to the mails under censorship rules.

My business was in jeopardy because an officer carelessly shouldered his authority. A short visit with him convinced me that his authority was now bordering on a dictatorial policy, which he alone was inaugurating.

"Anyone can see that 'So. Pacific' is giving our position away, telling the enemy right where we are," he explained to me.

The next day, I visited the base censor on Okinawa to explain my problem and to request his opinion. This man, whose colonel rank indicated that he was a senior postal inspector, was not one to be shoved around. His course of action was to take my name and my company address. Next, he asked for my commanding officer's name, after which I was dismissed with no hint of a future course of action.

The same week, two letters were torn in two and were returned to the writers. A note on the envelope by an officer stated, "Objectionable information enclosed, not mailable."

Encouraged by me, the writers took their letters to the base censor, asking for some intervention in the seemingly lordly ways of our company officers. The colonel promised the men he would act on their letters—a promise he kept. Again, he took their names and their addresses.

While my buddies were telling me about their visit, a visitor's jeep drove up and the colonel stepped out. He asked for the commanding officer, ordered a meeting of all officers immediately, and with the officers assembled, proceeded to outline their duties as censors. Gathered around the command post, we overheard the chewing our officers received from the colonel.

When the officers were dismissed from the meeting, the lieutenant came out a changed man!

"What can we write home, lieutenant?" someone asked.

"Any goddamn thing you want," was his reply.

That ended our censorship.

With new units coming ashore every day, the island looked like the Yankees were going to stay! It was a surprise to hear that an Army postal unit was coming ashore to set up a base post office. The unit turned out to be the same one in which many of us had worked in New York City, when we lived at Breslin Hotel on Twenty-ninth and Broadway.

With great expectations, we waited to see our old gang, who in due course came ashore with the bare necessities of life—a pup tent and a package of K-rations. We were set up in tents with all the conveniences of a permanent camp. They were thankful for the extra mattresses we gave them, because they wouldn't have to sleep on the ground.

During the course of coming ashore, Sharp (nicknamed "Not So Sharp" in New York), on touching the landing barge with his foot, felt secure enough to let go of the cargo net on which the men came down to board the barge. As a wave slid out from under the barge, Not So fell between the boat and the barge, getting the dunking of his life—followed by the ribbing of his life, after being pulled to safety!

* * *

Moving in the Army is a lesson in brevity—your tent is dropped, folded, and loaded on a DUKW, and on a release order, you are dispatched to the new camp area. On arrival you are assigned a new location, where the procedure is reversed—your tent is unloaded, unfolded, and raised.

Every GI became so accustomed to repetitious actions that it was second nature for someone to give a loud, encouraging, exclamatory order, "By the numbers!" Such an order relieved the tension, brought smiles, and burned into our short Army career a respect for Army formality. In a sense, we were the pioneers in this new and strange land, where we were helping make the laws that governed the island.

Our first payday was in sen and yen—ten sen equaled one yen; ten yen equaled one dollar. This was called occupation money and served us well in poker games. We were all of the opinion that since this was only

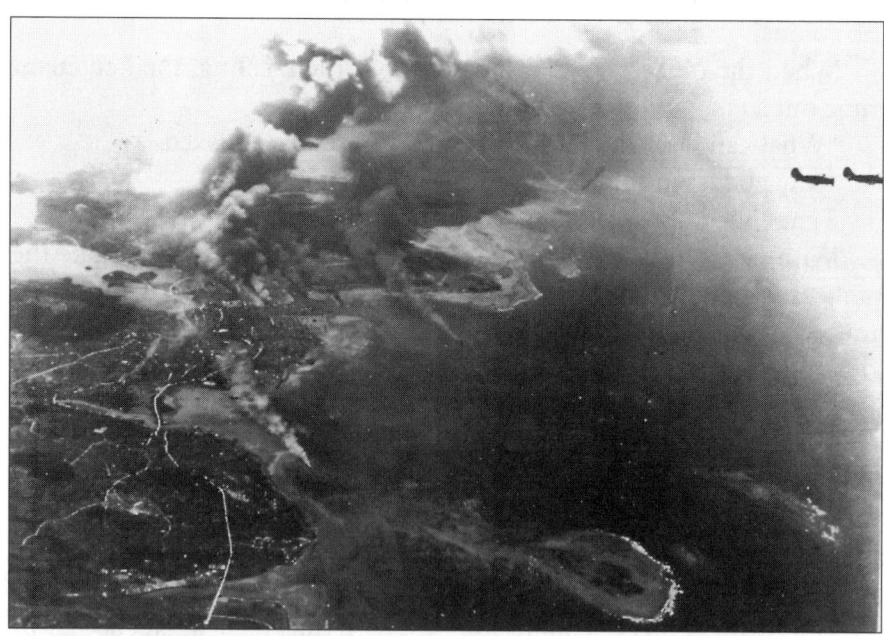

Harbor installations in Naha City, Okinawa Jaima, Ryukyu Retto, burning. Taken by a plane from USS Franklin CV-13, during Formosa Ryukyu strike.

play money, why not raise the bet? As usual, the good poker players were making out their money orders earlier than usual, since it took less time to win with bigger table stakes.

There was nothing to buy on Okinawa. There was no ice cream parlor, no neighborhood drugstore, no jewelry, and no souvenirs—in short, no stores whatsoever. What may have been stalls or shops were stripped of their contents by the natives as they left their villages, hiding their meager possessions in caves or crypts.

Summer was coming and the hard fighting was now centering around Naha and the southern end of Okinawa. Working at night, we could see the Marines' campfires and hear the guns firing from the many batteries set up on land. Going from our area to Naha, a distance of approximately ten miles, was like going into another world. During the day you could see combatants hunched over, following under the protective cover of a flamethrower tank, as they concentrated on a pillbox.

Here we were seeing the real mission of the Sherman tanks they had equipped with flamethrowers on the proving grounds of Pavuvu. Amazed as

Rifle sights lined on entrance to an Okinawa cave. Marines await result of an explosive charge to pick off any Japanese who attempt to excape. These caves formed the Japanese "Little Siegfried Line," defending the capital city of Naha.

111

we were when we first saw this stream of fire ejected toward an objective, we were even more impressed to see it in action. They were spewing flame seventy-five to 150 feet, as accurately as a fireman dispersing his nozzle of water while fighting a house fire.

Summer also brought the growing season, during which the natives cultivated their communal fields. Driving up to one of these fields, with forty to sixty natives on their knees or in various postures, we would stop and greet them with the only Japanese word we knew—"Ohio," which meant good morning. It was amazing to see the whole field of natives rise to full stature, repeat the greeting, then humbly bow. We would return their bow and drive off to our assignments—however, the courtesy was knocking down barriers.

This was the extent of our association until we started receiving boxes of chocolate bars containing wheat germ. This delicacy, intended to give a fighting man extra energy, had a peculiar hardness (to solve the heat problem of the Pacific), and an off-flavor taste. Nevertheless, these small bars made an impression on the Okinawa kids, who relished their flavor and no doubt benefited from their high nutritional value.

In our crude shower room, where two shower heads dispensed water supplied by an elevated pontoon section, the chips of remaining soap always disappeared. On walking to and from the showers, we often heard the giggling of girls, but never dreamed that they were scrutinizing us from the hedges surrounding parts of our camp. Our trips to the showers were made nude, with towels around our necks and shoes on our feet. Such nudity, at different times of the day, must have caused no end of mirth and amusement among the observers—the very ones who collected all the soap left in the showers!

It was a beautiful Fourth of July, so to commemorate the day, I dressed in a clean pair of fatigues; I even shined my shoes. After tidying up the tent and strapping my gas mask to the head of my cot, I joined a couple of buddies for a hike along the beach. We soon met a man who from the caduceus he was wearing, indicated he was from the medical corps, and was no doubt an officer. I saluted him, while my buddies brought their weapons down to a parade rest—a gesture of relief on their part, but impressive military courtesy as far as a colonel in the medical corps was concerned.

After a few bantered comments, we came right to the point and asked, "Sir, is it true that sixty-five percent of the women on Okinawa have VD, as they informed us when we were briefed for the invasion? Have you found any cases of VD?"

"No, we haven't found any VD on the island, but we had to tell you something to discourage fraternization," was his reply.

After the good doctor had taken leave, one of my buddies exclaimed, "Ya know, he thought you were an officer."

Glancing over their grubby-looking garb, I added, "It's amazing what clothes can do for a person!"

— Chapter IX —

Pacific War Ends

Summertime was passing. High-point GIs were grumbling about going back to the States, instead of going on the last invasion—the big push on the Island of Japan. No D-Day had been set, but the timetable indicated that it would be in the fall. Rumors kept trickling around camp that a new bomb had been dropped on Hiroshima. Perhaps these were well-founded rumors, for heavy security around the airport at Kadena indicated that some extra-special person or cargo was being handled.

Always, rumors reflect some semblance of reality. Unknown to every GI on the fighting front, President Truman gave his approval to use the atomic bomb. Carried by the bomber *Enola Gay*, the first A-bomb was dropped August 6, 1945. Hiroshima was shattered, with 92,000 people killed. On August 9, 40,000 died when the second bomb was dropped on Nagasaki.

We followed this devastation with wonderment and awe. Surely this atomic power was a strange new monster to be unleashed. We hoped it would end the war.

It was also Kar's fondest hope to escape the imminent invasion of Japan proper. He had little faith in the power and knee-buckling persuasion of the new atomic age. He held to his premise that a deaf soldier was of no value to the armed services. This logic was sound enough to those of us who felt sympathetic toward a GI who had grown weary of a trip that seemed sure to lead only to a cemetery. If not the enemy, surely the boredom and our own recklessness would eventually claim our souls.

Kar's ears were badly infected with a fungus that had started bothering him on Guadalcanal. "Damned if I don't get off this island," boasted Kar as he devised a scheme he conjured up from sheer ingenuity. "I'm reporting to sick bay and complain that I'm going deaf," he explained.

Sick bay's examination warranted further care than they could provide, so Kar was sent to the newly staffed Okinawa hospital, built with tents. Repeated injections in the buttocks with a sulfa drug caused more pain than relief for him. After a week, he confided to his GI visitors at the hospital that he had had enough needling in the rear, and that he was going to try to get released from the hospital so he could rejoin our company. Destiny has a strange way of changing plans. So it was with Kar.

Just as the bombing of Pearl Harbor started the war, a crackling announcement on August 10, 1945, ended the war. It was announced over the nine o'clock armed services news that the Emperor of Japan was interested in negotiating a peace treaty. Elation rocked the island. Bedlam broke loose as machine guns and antiaircraft guns spewed lead into the air, creating a fireworks that laced the sky with eerie streaks caused by the tracer bullets. Showgoers came running back to camp, shouting, "Head for your foxholes." Unmindful of the reason for the fireworks, they were naturally of the opinion we were being attacked.

Our victory was indecisive for several days as settlement terms were negotiated. Unconditional surrender was the term General MacArthur demanded and eventually received.

On August 10, when the fireworks were an instant reaction to the peace surrender announcement, Kar was stooped over his cot at the hospital, turning back his blankets in preparation for going to bed, when a fifty-caliber slug came ripping through the hospital tent. On the next visit to see Kar, tears were in his eyes as he showed us where the slug ripped a hole in his back.

"Now the war is over," lamented Kar, "and the doctor says I have to stay here till my wound heals. I'll never get home!"

The following poem, written on Okinawa at the end of the war, will rekindle the hardships experienced by the fighting men. May it serve as a spark to light new paths, no matter what your creed or where you live; no matter whether you are a soldier or a civilian seeking understanding and love.

Soldier be quick, be brave, be true,
Conquer these islands, democracy depends on you!
Through rain, through bullets, advance, advance,
Reckless your spirit, take one more chance.

There's no escaping, no softening of the raindrops' beat,
It's an endless challenge—a challenge all must meet.
Every cave, every hill, every pillbox a test,
Courageous their actions, till death gave them rest.
Hush! The sudden quiet comes a typhoon and rain,
Relentlessly challenging, defying those of us who remain,
Wind-twisted, shell—torn, yes, my heart sees it still,
Minds out of reason, in defense of this soldiers kill!
Somewhere back of the horizon blue,
Where the sunset tinges with a reddish hue,
Here lie the islands where cannibals once killed,
For the life taken, other stomachs were filled.
A matter of death, or a matter of life,
For the cannibal it was eternal strife.
What determinant can claim a life God gave?
Rightly, can anyone force a man to his grave?
Need we be killers one step improved?
Murder is murder when life is removed.
Let agitated ripples for lasting peace
Swell to rolling breakers, that wars may cease!

* * *

With the war's end, a slow shock wave hit the front fighting men. It was a warming thrill to see some of the released prisoners of war, held in Japanese prison camps, filter through Okinawa. When they came to our coconut-log theatre in the open clearing, with a movie screen on the downhill end of the theatre, the fighting men would rise in groups to surrender seats to the released POWs.

To the winners should go the spoils of victory! Our reaction was now that the war is over, there's no damned sense in hard work, it's time for a letdown!

In a short time baseball gloves, bats, and balls showed up. Rusty as they were, athletes started playing, displaying their various degrees of cleverness. Mine was the faking of catching a ball with the left hand, letting the ball slip by, and then catching it with the right hand held close to the chest. Poor judgment of the speed of a knuckleball I attempted to catch broke a finger on my right hand. Lurt Fully broke two bones in his first game and was sent to Guam for treatment. He was one of the first of our 454th Company to leave Okinawa.

Shortly, calls for high-point men released others from the company to head for the States.

Interestingly enough, barriers between the natives and the GIs were removed and the fraternization order was overlooked.

It was a fall day when Sergeant Holly from the Air Corps came visiting me and suggested we try our luck initiating love affairs with some native Okinawans. Such a challenge was soon met with a quick shave and a change into clean GI trousers—the only dressing decision a GI ever made.

We were off to Yanaabaru, where a large concentration of natives had set up housekeeping. As we walked down a dusty road, we confronted a group of women expressing great anxiety, looking over their shoulders and muttering distressed tones bordering on whimperings.

"Something's wrong," said Holly. "Wonder what it is?"

We hailed the women, who then stopped in their tracks, not knowing what to do. They were scared of what they were running from, and timid about being in our presence. Holly, six feet four inches tall, was indeed a giant to be reckoned with by these five-foot-four-inch and five-foot-five-inch women. They muttered in their native language for a time, and then came up with the words "push-push," shaking their heads negatively and pointing in the direction from which they had come.

"Somebody is trying to make out," said Holly, sitting down and lighting a cigarette.

"I'll walk them through the danger area and see that they are not molested," I said, starting off and motioning for the women to follow.

They followed, talking hurriedly in Japanese about their common danger. Their concern was that of being raped. Once through the wooded area, we came into view of the rolling, open country down to the water's edge, where they could see their community across a narrow patch of water that could be waded across at low tide.

Deep bows of thanks were my reward for safely delivering them. Many words of Japanese followed, but fell on unrecording ears. Smiles indicated their pleasure. My departure was that of a gentleman for, after all, they were unfortunate souls who had been through much, and who undoubtedly had lost their sweethearts or husbands, and were not to be taken advantage of by a GI.

Returning to where I had left Holly, I was amazed that he had not only met two women, but had loved one of them.

"Incredible, I just don't believe it! Not in the little time that I've been gone, which was less than one hour. Are you telling me the truth?"

"Here's the tissue paper I cleaned up with," said Holly, taking six strides off the road into a beautiful grassy clearing, and pointing to the ground.

His evidence was overwhelming, and the situation induced the two of us to relieve ourselves. As we were bouncing the tissue around with our well-directed streams, we were greeted with the girlish giggles of the two women he had met.

We eventually spotted them on the ridge of the clearing, half hidden by bushes they were sitting between. Holly and I rejoined the girls, who were most receptive to our advances, but asked us to get them some food.

Fortunately, in the neighborhood was the First Engineer Battalion. We were given K-rations by the mess hall sergeant, when we explained our bargaining position. He replied to our thanks by calling out, "You lucky moochers!"

It was a foursome picnic on this most memorable day on Okinawa. As the evening's hush fell over the countryside, I was to learn about the tenderness, charm, and the amazing subtle moves possessed by my newest acquaintance.

Having eaten, she took her jacket off and gently spread it over our heads, bringing us together. Gently she pressed her lips to mine and gave me the first loving kiss I had had in two years. Emboldened, I took her head between my two hands and held it in position to look into her pleading soft brown eyes. As she turned away she took one of the cigarettes from the K-ration box, drew up the jacket more snugly, then carefully lit the cigarette, making sure that the light would not reveal our location. Her first puff taken, she held the cigarette to my lips. Together we shared.

Never having kissed an Oriental, I was thrilled to find that her responses were as impulsive as mine. Togetherness was driving us to greater familiarity. Without a single inhibition I kissed her breast and noted the pleasant aroma of the stateside toilet soap she used.

After our second climax, she took complete charge and ever so tenderly placed me in proper position for an Oriental loving that finalized all a lover could ask. Following a very close-together rest time, she and I started to leave, followed by Holly and his friend. She was leading, holding my hand. All was quiet, with darkness a bottomless pit.

Suddenly she froze in her tracks, pulled my head down to hers, and electrified me with the whispered word "Nipponese!" She pointed my arm in a direction that would take us to the First Engineer Battalion, kissed me tenderly for the last time, squeezed my hand as a loving gesture, and slipped away with her friend into a blackness that suited the ending to so many of my nocturnal emissions—the curse of overseas duty.

Holly unhesitatingly followed me, and shortly we saw a light in the distance. Once at the First Engineer Battalion we would be out of the woods and onto a highway, which would eventually get us home. Even though the war was officially over, not all Nipponese were well informed of the fact, so confrontations were to be avoided.

On the highway our objective was to hitchhike a ride back to Holly's camp. Consequently, the first set of headlights approaching revealed four arms held above our heads. The truck never slowed. We commenced waving to attract attention, but to no avail. Jumping off the road to avoid being run over, we were amazed to see the brake lights flash on, and to hear the brakes squeal as the truck came to a stop. When Holly and I started to climb into the cab, a black man exclaimed, "I sure didn't want to be stopped by no Japanese. Glad to see that you all are GIs."

On the way home, Holly said he had a fifth of whiskey at camp, which would help cleanse our mouths and make the evening a memorable one. The driver delivered us to the Air Corps base. Holly's buddies soon promoted a party as they listened to our day's experience. The fifth of whiskey was followed by a batch of raisin jack, brewed by some of the airmen.

We were on the last of a case of beer when Holly asked the driver of a water tanker to take me back to my company area. Willingly and with a feeling of camaraderie, the driver, Holly, Frank (another airman), and I jumped in the front seat of the water tanker, with a beer in our hands to enjoy along the way. Few times in my life had I mixed drinks and stayed sober to tell about it. This night of nights, I was feeling as though I could solve the world's problems with love alone.

Peacefully I watched as a curve in the road appeared, and the driver sat motionless behind the steering wheel. In fact, no one commented on the impending danger of driving a GI truck off the road into a twenty-foot embankment. Looking at the driver's face, I realized that his reflexes were numbed by alcohol. In fact, the ensuing accident proved that his mind was also at rest! His response to the accident was, "What happened?"

Fortunately no one was killed. Our truck crashed into the embankment on the curve. The water tank, in the bed of the GI truck, sailed over the cab of the truck.

Frank, the other airman going for the ride, was badly squeezed when the door sprang open on impact, and he fell between the truck and the embankment. His hospitalization was three days inasmuch as he was unable to pass water.

Army military police brought the remaining three of us to the sick bay, which was in our area. After pronouncing the driver inebriated, which didn't require a doctor's degree, the good doctor patched up a number of abrasions and cuts.

Holly and I then asked for a prophylactic.

"A what?" exclaimed the doctor.

"A 'pro,'" said Holly. "You know, a preventative to keep from getting a venereal disease."

"You've been out with those nurses who got here last month," said the doctor assumptively. Then he added, with a defeatist attitude, "I haven't been able to touch them with a ten-foot pole, and I work with them!"

— Chapter X —

Typhoon
October 9–11, 1945

When your whole company is ordered to secure its operation be cause of a typhoon, you sense an impending danger—one that is gigantic and awesome, and gives no quarter. Clouds were riding high and moving rapidly, spreading over more and more sky as the whole island was covered by a pall that made midday seem a late evening dusk. Vehicle drivers were hurrying along with their jeeps, trucks, and DUKWs to make it back to camp before the typhoon was to strike, which was sometime around 6 P.M.

Pulling into our area, the sergeants ordered the drivers to move the DUKWs alongside their tents.

"Tie down your tents to your DUKW—lower your tent flaps—drive additional stakes."

GI buddies were busy trenching around their tents to keep the water from seeping into our living rooms. Weights like stones, spare tires, and heavy timbers were laid on our tent flaps to hold them down. Our sergeant's orders were followed and additional stakes were driven with additional ropes added to secure the tents.

"Damn if it doesn't look like rain," said Prop, as the trees were being blown back and forth like wheat in a field.

A lightness of air pressure made you feel as though you were walking in a semi-vacuum. It was a gradual backing off of air to be replaced by a wind, the likes of which we had never experienced in our travels through the South Pacific. Like mothers, our tent mates were relieved to welcome home the last of the GIs to report to their quarters. From them came a final report of the outside world. Quonset huts were being blown apart with a near miss, as one airborne sheet of metal nearly hit the speaker, who was excitedly giving the typhoon report.

Confronted by a new enemy, dismay and disbelief gripped our whole company as our tents began to blow apart. Gusts of wind would partially collapse the tent, then a puff would balloon it. Tents were acting crazy—laboriously breathing like an exhausted runner fighting for air. This beating would cause the sewn seams to pull apart with a gnashing rip that would expose the occupants and all their possessions to the fury of the storm. Grabbing their most prized belongings—a girlfriend's picture and their duffel bag—they would double up with a buddy and his tent mates.

Getting through the tent flaps of a befriending neighbor was a problem, as those inside were having trouble keeping the wind from finding any sizeable opening. Once you made a mistake with a gust of wind, your tent was gone! Our DUKWs were nobly serving as wind breakers, as well as anchors to which we tied our tents. Otherwise our losses would have been another Army-recorded tragedy.

The next day, October 10, our camp was groaning like a feverish patient. Winds still ripped tents apart! Loosening the tent ropes kept the ever-shrinking ropes from pulling our stakes out of the ground. Boards to stand on were gathered from any available source. A blown-down tent was soon stripped for any protection it afforded. Mud clung to boots; even the ground inside our tents became a gumbo which had to be scraped off with our large Marine knives. Going to the mess hall was uncalled for, as no one ventured from a livable tent as long as there was food inside. Besides, a fire inside with eight or ten GIs seemed a cozy circumstance.

Separating our camp area from our latrine (an outhouse with eight holes) was a sizeable depression at least a hundred yards across. With the heavy rains, this depression filled with water and eventually became a small river, necessitating the driving of a DUKW to and from the latrine. Arriving at the eight-holer you had to stand on the seat, for the water table had forced millions of maggots to crawl topside, literally covering the floor and seating areas an inch in depth with their writhing bodies. Hourly a horn would sound and a voice would announce "latrine run," and those waiting could climb aboard for the most unique bathroom facilities in the South Pacific!

By October 11 our conditions improved; wind and rain became bearable. Our C-rations were augmented with fresh potatoes and fresh eggs, which were fortunately foraged from the first fresh rations to arrive on Okinawa. We had started unloading transports just before they were ordered to pull out of the harbor because of the typhoon alarm. How this food trickled into our area was never questioned, but it was far superior to the dehydrated potatoes and powdered eggs, which had been a mainstay on our menus for the past two years. It was a pleasing picture to see tents full of GIs idly enjoying a forced break.

"How come you ever wound up in the Army, Alex?" asked Prop as he was peeling potatoes.

Kar, a husky six-foot-two-inch, two-hundred-ten-pound Pennsylvanian of Polish descent, was pumping air into one of two blowtorches. "Just as soon as I get our two torches set up to heat this five-gallon can of water to boil these three dozen fresh eggs, you'll hear my story," he answered.

By cutting away one side of a five-gallon can one inch from the top and bending it inward, the heat from the blowtorches was deflected upward to a grill. Perched on the grill was the five-gallon can, containing water and eggs, alluded to by Kar.

Kar sat on a bed nearest to the blowtorches, pulled his boots from the mud, plunked them down on a board, looked at Prop, and said, "You'll never believe me, but I was drafted."

"How could a patriotic man like you keep from volunteering?" asked Prop.

"Yeah," said another. "Look how good Uncle treats you—and with fresh potatoes and eggs!"

"But I never wanted to be a soldier," replied Kar. "I had always worked in a meat market. In fact, I was the head mixer and stuffer of Polish sausages where I worked. I met lots of nice people, loved my job, and got good wages. Then came Pearl Harbor. Naturally, making sausages was a nonessential job as far as the armed services were concerned, so I decided to get into defense-oriented work where you could have a deferment, because of your civilian contribution to the war effort.

"I went to Pittsburgh and got a job in the steel mill. They gave me the hardest and hottest job in the whole plant. Nightly I would come home too tired to eat, with cramps and pains in every muscle of my body. My back ached whether I stood, sat, or laid down. My only comforting thought was that some day my body would become conditioned to the hard work, and I would have no more suffering. My mother was the only person wholly in agreement with my plan.

"However, no sooner did I learn my job, with the mental and physical adjustments made, than I received a letter from the President. It was the first time he knew I was alive! Truthfully, the draft board had me in the Army before I got my first paycheck from the steel mill, and here I am!

"Who wants a soft-boiled egg?" concluded Kar.

Naturally as many hands responded as there were bodies. Soon a can of beer appeared for each, a deck of cards was asked for, and a five-cent bet-limit game of poker commenced.

Potatoes were boiled and then fried in our mess gear, tasting like home-cooked hash browns made with loving care. Another cook followed with eggs fried to anyone's liking.

Prop was asked how he had come to be in the Army, and with his best Georgian drawl, he came up with the damnedest story for volunteering ever heard.

"It was like this," he said. "I loved this sweet little neighbor girl and could hardly stay away from her place. Her daddy had me helping around the farm. Well, the last job I had was running a caterpillar for him. I was leveling some farm land when I saw him coming across the field, at which time I jumped off the caterpillar and headed for the nearest recruiting office."

At this point he cut his story.

"Rube, did that girl love you?" asked a tent mate, wanting to extract the last amour from any romantic story.

"Oh yes," said Prop. "In fact, she loved me too much and got pregnant, and that was the reason her daddy was coming to see me."

Another pause occurred.

"What happened?" asked another buddy.

"As far as I know that caterpillar is still running," concluded Prop.

While boiling another five-gallon can full of eggs—for passing the time as well as for preparing an instant treat for anyone who might drop in for a visit—the story of how the eggs were procured was told.

On October 8, while the regular crew was hauling eggs ashore, a DUKW was taken from the motor pool and fell in line to bring ashore a load. Once it was loaded with two sling loads of eggs (each sling contained fifteen cases), it proceeded to an undisclosed, unlighted, unchartered section of the beach. It was a nighttime operation calling for the most in amphibious maneuvering. It was an operation testing the driver's ability to move a vehicle over unseen obstacles, not only coral reefs coming out of the water, but uneven terrain that could cause a wreck.

Without a word spoken, the driver and his buddy came ashore. They were well up the beach when they faintly recognized a white coral ribbon, indicative of a road, toward which they steered their vehicle.

A triumphant feeling of having accomplished an impossible mission was settling over the two when they were brought to their senses of reality with a shouted "Halt!"

Stopping as if they had encountered Saint Peter at the Golden Gate, they sat perfectly still, not knowing what to think of their predicament.

"What ya all got here?" asked one of the Marine outpost guards, as he climbed the DUKW and flashed a light on the cargo.

"Eggs," answered the driver.

"Ya mind giving us a case?" asked the guard.

"Take two—one apiece, just tell us how the hell to get to the traffic circle," was the driver's relieved reply.

The cases of eggs were well worth the exchange of directions given, and the rest of the cargo got to camp without further incident and was hurriedly distributed to everyone. An inspection the next day could not locate an egg! The recipients found safe hiding places for over 10,000 eggs—hiding them in brush, culverts, crypts, and in the company supply room. It was the first successful egg hunt on Okinawa—happening approximately six months after our D-Day landing on Easter Sunday, April 1, 1945.

Okinawa's typhoon was a battle against the elements. Facts that have been recorded indicate that the wind velocity was 132 miles per hour, that 127 naval vessels were damaged or beached, that 1,250 hospital patients needed to be relocated to Guam when hospitals were damaged, that port facilities were reduced to a litter of splintered wreckage; and that pontoon docks were washed ashore and communications destroyed. China clipper planes were torn from moorings and also washed ashore. Everywhere damage was visible, but the tireless GIs hastily replaced the unserviceable equipment; ten-in-one rations arrived via plane. The Army reported one hundred casualties and the Navy reported eighty-nine deaths.

* * *

Jack Stole, a private who made good in the Army Postal Battalion in New York City, was with the Army postal base post office, which had moved from New York to Okinawa.

Many of the amphibious truck drivers had been Army postal workers in New York before being replaced by a WAC (Women's Army Corps) and transferred into either the European theatre or the Asiatic-Pacific theatre of operations. Stole had stayed on with the postal battalion and had become a master sergeant before arriving on Okinawa. Naturally, we had many pleasant remembrances to talk over with our old friends, who were now handling the mail for the last big post office of the Pacific.

As drivers, we befriended our postal coworkers in many ways and always kept their welfare foremost in our various assignments. Whatever they needed, we made it a point to supply. So, it was no surprise that, with the end of the war and the typhoon, some of our close postal friends and the Army DUKW drivers who had worked previously together in New York decided to have a party.

Getting the beer was the problem. However, some observant DUKW driver knew that a barge full of beer was down on the dock by the Ishikawa River. With five seashell souvenirs, we went down to buy beer. At first, the guards were reluctant. Nevertheless, after we explained the reason for the party and they recognized old combatants deserving an overseas fling, they took another look at the beautiful pin souvenirs we offered and gave us three cases of beer.

We got our beer delivered in a barracks bag to our four-by-four truck, where six of us planted our feet on it. The driver was about to drive off when, unknown to us, a detachment of black SPs were suspicious of us and made a search of our vehicle. On finding the barracks bag full of beer, they divided us into two groups, and were going to take us to the Naval Operations Base. Jack, Buddy G, a DUKW driver, and I were in one truck driven by a black driver. The others, with the beer, were in our truck driving ahead of us—leading the parade, so to speak, to a beer bust that was never to be!

As we approached the traffic circle, a shot was fired. Stole and I saw the flash. A fast response by the driver brought the truck to a screeching halt. The momentum of Buddy G and the guard catapulted the two off the truck and into the ditch, as a second shot was fired and lit up the night.

My immediate response was to stop the fight that was in progress between my buddy and the shore patrolman. As I jumped off the truck an inner voice said, "Stay away, get back on the truck." A light went on as if God spoke. As I started to climb on the truck, a third shot was fired. The top man in the ditch stopped beating the man he was sitting on and slowly slumped forward.

The fighting was over. The man on top was dead, bleeding from a shot that had struck him between the eyes.

Buddy G was helped from the ditch, having received one of his worst beatings of the war.

We were then ordered into the truck for the completion of our trip to the Naval Operations Base. Fearing that the fatal shooting would push the shore patrolman into further atrocities for vengeance, we all refused, saying that we wanted a military policeman to clear us from the scene of outright manslaughter, since we were Army personnel. We were conceded our point and waited at the scene until a jeep with two MPs drove up to take us to the Naval Operations Base.

We, as well as the SP, were being interrogated by the naval officer. At one point an ensign said that we should be given an alcoholic test to see if we drank too much, and if we were telling the truth. One of the group members then gave the grand hailing sign of distress, and while everyone pondered the utterance of such phraseology, the lieutenant commander picked up the utterance for its meaning and ordered that due to the lateness of the hour, the prisoners be fed and that the shore patrol be secured for the night.

It was 6 A.M. when our company commander came to the shore patrol's office to pick us up. He never asked us what had happened, nor did he judge us harshly. His only order was that we were under company arrest and henceforth could not leave the company area.

We were watching the high-point men leave in ever-increasing numbers. Alex Kar was, at long last, to leave the island on a ship that had agreed to take six GIs back to the States as soon as they were given clearance from the island commander. Six of our 454th DUKW drivers were approved by the company commander, and Kar was one of the lucky ones. However, when the island commander was giving his clearance, the ship was asked if it had passage for any GIs.

"Yes, sir," was the reply, "and we have them aboard."

"Remove them," ordered the island commander. "We'll tell you who is to leave this island!"

When Kar returned to our tent, his tears proved the old saying, "Never watch a man cry." It was pathetic to see a grown man, so deeply involved with his battle to return home, break up emotionally when he was rejected for returning to the States—even after the war was over!

As men of our company started to be shipped home, there were sad farewells and promises to write and keep in touch. Say hello to your mother who made us all the cookies. Another favorite was say hello to your sweetheart who wrote us all those sexy letters.

Commented Jolly Robers, who was obsessed with a hatred for Army regimentation, "I wouldn't take a million bucks for my experience, but I wouldn't go through it again for ten million!"

It was late November and since I was restricted to the company area, it was impossible to sell my seashell souvenirs. With a little help, I made contact with some Air Force personnel who became my organized sales force. They were buying the pins I made for a twenty percent discount, paying eight dollars for my ten-dollar item. Marvel at Yankee ingenuity— my amazing salesmen raised the price to fifteen dollars, and in three days they had sold every last pin I had made.

My goal to make a pin for every cross in the Guadalcanal cemetery was fulfilled—over fourteen hundred crosses were made on my trek through the forward area.

It was Stole who was the first to receive a court-martial for the killing of the shore patrolman. Anxiety had built for two weeks, as various investigations were made. On the day of the court-martial I was visited by Jack, now a free man; all charges were dismissed. As Jack told me, the driver of the truck had finally admitted at the court-martial that it was he who stopped the truck, jumped out with his carbine, ran to the rear of the truck and from that position shot at the top man, killing him instantly.

It was another week before the rest of us were tried and released. When I received my summary court-martial, the officer explained that this formality had to be followed so that no further civilian action could ever be taken. With that pronouncement, he pointed to the barracks bag and said, "You may take the evidence with you."

The three cases of beer that had been in the barracks bag had by now been reduced to six cans!

It was a tremendous relief to have such a weight lifted from our shoulders. With the war won and with the court-martial case cleared, we could sail home from the Pacific claiming somewhat of a personal victory.

I was the last driver in our company to proudly drive a DUKW from our location on Easy Street to the island motor pool, where the war machinery for the South Pacific had their switches turned off for the last time.

These machines—the amtracs, the DUKWs, the trucks, and the jeeps—were a tribute to the American people and their productivity. The individuals who drove them were a fraternity of men who held the war effort together by keeping the fighting men supplied and bringing the sick and the casualties back for medical help.

It was at my first American Legion convention, when the colorful Drum and Bugle Corps competed for the championship, that I realized how proud I was to have served my country through the battle of the South Pacific.

When "The Star-Spangled Banner" was played, my eyes closed on the scene before me and I was once again in the South Pacific with my old Army buddies, watching the bombs bursting in air, and waiting for another day…just another day! It would have brought tears to their eyes as it did mine.

There are two worlds—the one in which we live and the idealistic one of which we dream. Stretching out across the Pacific Ocean, our efforts laid a cornerstone in the idealistic world. Those we came in contact with could start building a new world, where human rights could become a reality.

Individually and collectively, it is the capabilities of the GIs in the driver's seat that determine the final outcome of what happens on the battlefield. Given a job they will find a way to do it.

In retrospect I would like to say that the Marine combatants are the greatest. Let these words of praise also extend to the Army, Navy, and Air Corps.

THE SECRETARY OF THE NAVY

WASHINGTON

The President of the United States
takes pleasure in presenting the

PRESIDENTIAL UNIT CITATION
To the
FIRST MARINE DIVISION (REINFORCED)

Consisting of FIRST Marine Division; First Amphibian Tractor Battalion, FMF; U.S. Navy Flamethrower Unit Attached; Sixth Amphibian Tractor Battalion (Provisional), FMF; Third Armored Amphibian Battalion (Provisional), FMF; Detachment Eighth Amphibian Tractor Battalion, FMF; 454th Amphibian Truck company, U.S. Army; 456th Amphibian Truck Company, U.S. Army; Fourth Joint Assault Signal Company, FMF; Fifth Separate Wire Platoon, FMF; Sixth Separate Wire Platoon, FMF. for service as set forth in the following

CITATION:
"For extraordinary heroism in action against enemy Japanese Forces at Peleliu and Ngesebus from September 15 to 29, 1944. Landing over a treacherous coral reef against hostile mortar and artillery fire, the First Marine Division, Reinforced, seized a narrow, heavily mined beachhead and advanced foot by foot in the face of relentless enfilade fire through rain forests and mangrove swamps toward the air strip, the key to the enemy defenses of the Southern Palaus. Opposed all the way by thoroughly disciplined, veteran Japanese troops heavily entrenched in caves and in reinforced concrete pillboxes which honeycombed the high ground throughout the island, the officers and men of the Division fought with undiminished spirit and courage despite heavy losses, exhausting heat and difficult terrain, seizing and holding a highly strategic air and land base for future operations in the Western Pacific. By their individual acts of heroism, their aggressiveness and their fortitude, the men of the First Marine Division, Reinforced, upheld the highest traditions of the United States Naval Service."

For the President,
(Sgd) Frank Knox
Secretary of the Navy

HEADQUARTERS
454TH AMPHIBIAN TRUCK COMPANY
KADENA, OKINAWA
1 October 1945
Names of Attached Men

Allpress, Lauten E.
Asbury, Edgar H.
Auwen, Fred L.

Baca, Bences
Bandura, Andrew
Baranowski, Joseph N.
Barfield, Arthur L.
Barkley, Billy
Batchelder, Bertram A.
Bentz, Ralph L.
Berntsen, Douglas C.
Bisson, Chester F.
Blakemore, Russell
Bludman, Hyman
Bowerman, Foster L.
Brekka, Walter
Brennfleck, Edward A.
Brewer, Dean H.
Bronemann, LeRoy B.
Bronson, Uriel E.
Brown, Harold G.
Brunst, Robert W.
Burkiewicz, Robert E.
Buterbaugh, George W.

Carter, Paul E.

Chadima, Edwin L.
Cheatham, Lewis F.
Cheslock, Michael
Cirofici, Anthony
Clevinger, Beecher
Cole, Gilbert D.
Connsoliver, Noah
Cooper, Donald C.
Corbin, Roy J.
Cramer, Harry W.
Criscione, Paul J.
Crown, Bernard
Culver, Alvin E.
Cymanski, Frank J.

Davis, Philip A.
Deebo, Edward
Deel, Garfield
Densmore, Churchill
DePew, Harold E., Jr.
Difazio, Vincent A.
Donlon, John H.
Dooley, George J.
Drahus, Michael
Drewniak, Wladyslaw
Driscoll, Timothy
Dry, Edward H.
Dugan, Robert E.

Eairlieywine, Donald L.

Faloona, James
Farley, William J.
Farmer, William T.
Fleming, Olin B.
Forsythe, Arthur R.
Freeberg, Keith F.
Fulkerson, Albert W.

Giles, Raymond C.
Glaskey, Chester T.
Goetz, Harold R.
Gore, Milton C.
Gosnell, Charles R.
Gregoire, Adrian A.
Gretchco, Adam
Griswold, Percy R., Jr.
Gurganus, William

Haas, Thomas
Haines, John A.
Hale, Raymond L.
Hartl, Alois
Held, George W.
Hendrix, George J.
Hennington, Gordon E.
Hinkle, Jess W.
Hodges, Carl J., Jr.
Hollenbaugh, John H.
Horwat, Joseph, Jr.
Howell, Emmett
Huddle, James V.
Hutton, Carl S.

Isbell, James D.

Johnson, John E.
Johnson, Robert L.
Jordan, Carroll L.
Jurries, Harold H.

Kachmarsky, Andrew
Kanar, Alexandria S.
Karcher, Norman F.
Kennedy, Bruce G.
Kinkead, Alfred J.
Krol, Henry M.

Landon, Howard A.
Landon, Raymond J.
Lawson, Harry E.
Lohrman, Ernest A.
Long, William A.
Loveridge, Ernest L.
Lynch, Joseph J.

Macquire, John E.
Mahoney, Francis J.
Martinez, Salvador
Martini, Salvatore A.
Marzka, Lorence W.
Mathis, Jack E.
Maudsley, William, Jr.
McCaffrey, Edward F.
McClosky, Louis W.
McClung, Bronson D.
McCool, Luke A.
McCurdy, Eddie
McKim, Major M.
McKoon, James R.
McLean, Ennis
Mehle, Robert G.

Michael, William H.

Mick, John P.

Miller, Ernest H.

Mohun, Edward J.

Nahem, Morris

Nannini, James

Olson, Harry N.

Orszulak, Steve F.

Ottinger, Alden B.

Parson, Isaac W.

Pease, Joe P.

Pecker, Sol

Perreault, Angelo J.

Petch, Harold B.

Philo, Alvin C.

Prophett, Ruben J. T.

Pulley, Lurton

Quigley, James G.

Rall, Richard E.

Richter, Arthur L.

Riggins, Oscar L.

Robinson, Robert D.

Roew, Frederick, Jr.

Rogers, Charles F.

Russell, Raymond H.

Rutkowski, Chester

Sabo, George

Schwarz, Max

Shafer, Monzel F.

Shelton, John H.

Shenberger, Earl L.

Simonson, Albert R.

Slasko, John J.

Sledge, J. M.

Smith, Carl C.

Smith, Raymond B.

Sobieck, Kurt A.

Spears, Harry E.

St. Clair, Wallace C.

Stachowski, Stephen W.

Stair, McKindrey L.

Stewart, Roderick

Sullivan, Vincent J. A.

Sundall, Gilbert R.

Susso, Anthony S.

Sutton, George F.

Swingle, Leo C.

Talcove, Neil

Tatum, George A.

Thaxton, Elwood

Tortes, Frank

Trautman, Raymond H.

Traylor, James E.

Troute, William

Turpin, Clyde W.

Ulz, Joseph

Verbeck, Thomas J.

Wanick, Allard L.

Wasilewski, Theodore A.

Weimer, Raymond C.

White, John J.

Once Upon a Tide

White, William J.
Wilhauk, Marcel J.
Williams, Howard W.
Wilson, Russel R.
Wood, Howard A.
Woodson, Larence W.

Zeper, Louis

Officers

Biggers, W. G.
Clark, Fred F.
Corbin, John
Culver, Arthur L.
Stinson, R. C.
Wakefield, Olis M.
Yancey, J. H.

Introduction to the Appendix

The author, in full combat uniform, stands by the foxhole built to accommodate him and his tent mates.

Appendix

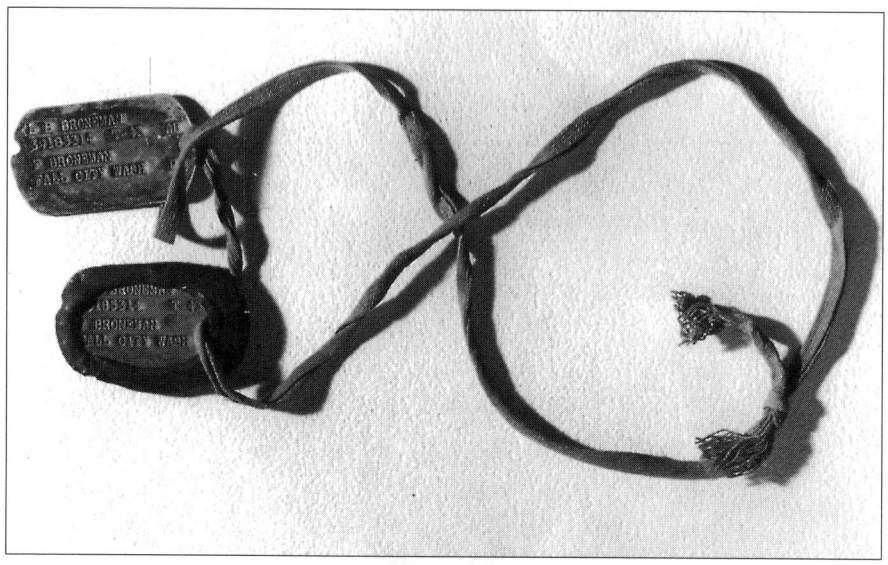

Semper Fidelis
(Always faithful-Motto of the U.S. Marine Corps.) Proudly these dog tags returned after 27 months in a forward area (810 days - 1620 changes in the tides)!

Dreams do come true! In marriage you seek a helpmate, one who loves you and shares your goals. Sweethearts are severely tested. This was especially true of those who had boyfriends overseas. Those who stood the test were married as the servicemen returned.

Lillie was the consummate helpmate. All I accomplished in the service can be credited to her love, patience and competence. Yes, we were married. Our love blossomed anew as her role increased from helpmate to mother, then to my guiding light as we became involved in community activities.

Her capabilities seemed limitless because of her interest in what I had experienced during the war. We started planning a trip to the South Pacific. When I retired from the post office after thirty-eight and a half years, our plans became a reality. Twenty-six thousand miles and three months later, we had revisited the islands where the 454th Amphibious Truck Company had been stationed.

Yes, there were moments when I was gently touched by the memories of incidents involving men who are living, as well as those who have long since died. It was my singular footstep that often walked the beach where the vehicles of our invasion force once roared.

Tides ebb and flow, sands shift, goals become altered, ideals may lose focus, but my Army sweetheart Lillie faithfully contributed as my helpmate to all that I hold dear. Thanks again to Lillie for having made this dream book possible. I invite you to revisit the islands with us in the appendix, as Lillie reports on our 1979 trip.

Privately yours,
LeRoy B. Bronemann

Preface to the Appendix

Inasmuch as my husband has been so generous in giving me much credit for my part in his life, I feel that it is important that I share with you the following pages of a memorable trip. It is one we will never forget, and we hope that someday soon we may be able to retrace our steps.

We realized that this would be the experience of a lifetime. LeRoy had been in the South Pacific for twenty-seven months and during that time, I had been working in New York City, cutting out all the articles on the war's progress in that area in each day's newspaper. He had been through it physically, and yet I followed all the naval engagements and bombardments so closely that I knew where he was going before he arrived there.

Going to the South Pacific seemed only natural, since in order to write *Once upon a Tide,* we felt we had to be there to relive the anxiety, experiences, and humorous times that existed thirty-six years before. In addition there was a natural desire to return to the South Pacific (the islands, campsites, and people) to see exactly how it was today. We will try to explain each visit as we saw it.

In all the years we have been married I don't believe that anything has stirred us more. To search for a combat area, to find where a beach was invaded, to actually step on the ground where your company camped, to relive the horrors of war, and to remember where you lost one of your best buddies are most touching experiences.

There were days when we worked very hard to find but one clue which would lead us to a particular spot. However, once that spot was reached and we realized that this was the place back in 1943, 1944, or 1945, the tears could not be retained. It is most touching when you stand at such a spot and thank God that you were fortunate to survive it all. Yet you feel very humble for having the privilege of being able to return.

Appendix

There were many times, after seeing the rugged terrain on Guadalcanal and Peleliu, that I wondered how our fighting men were able to overcome the many obstacles that they encountered. I feel that if everyone had the opportunity to see these battlefields, no more wars would be necessary—the horrors of them would be forever implanted on one's mind. It is actually hard to write these experiences, inasmuch as you relive the findings on every island, rekindling sparks of diverse emotions.

We civilians owe a deep debt of gratitude to all our servicemen who serve and have served these great United States of ours!

It is hoped therefore that the following pages, which are a daily diary of our true experiences, will be not only educational but enjoyable to our readers, and especially to the servicemen who served in the Pacific Theatre during World War II.

Noumea, New Caledonia

On February 23, 1979, LeRoy and I left Seattle for a three-month trip through the South Pacific to revisit the battle areas where he had been during the war and also the areas he had been in prior to the invasions.

Therefore, the main areas to be visited were New Caledonia, Guadalcanal, Peleliu, and Okinawa. A tentative itinerary was made, air tickets purchased, hotel reservations made, and length of time we would be on each island estimated, and unbelievably, we did not alter our course once we got started.

From Seattle we flew via Honolulu to Tahiti, Moorea, and Bora Bora, then to Rarotonga in the Cook Islands, then to Fiji, and after a marvelous month we were ready to settle down and proceed with our mission.

On Thursday morning, March 22, we arrived at Tontouta Airport on New Caledonia. The bus ride into Noumea took 45 minutes. Immediately after checking into our hotel, we signed up for a 2 P.M. city tour in order to get oriented. Noumea is built on hills and you can get a spectacular view from any one of them. The museum, located in the downtown area, was our last stop, so we remained in that area to reconfirm our onward trip to the New Hebrides.

That must have been a lucky move for us! In the airline ticket office we met a young gentleman who worked in the library at the South Pacific Commission. We handed him one of our cards showing the South Pacific Seashell Cross and LeRoy in full combat uniform. We explained that we were doing research for our book, and were interested in meeting someone who may have been in Noumea during World War II, and who would know where the various armed forces of the United States had been stationed.

Appendix

He suggested we come to the South Pacific commission where he would introduce us to a woman who had worked for the South Pacific Area Engineers of the United States during the war.

The following morning we were introduced to the woman, who gave us a background of the area and informed us that very few people lived in Noumea during the war—most of the natives were with their tribes throughout the island. She suggested that we contact Henri Daly, who worked in a downtown department store and was well informed about the American activities on New Caledonia.

We phoned Daly for an appointment, but he was not in his office at that time. Stores and all businesses close for two hours in the middle of each day, so when we did not receive a return call by noon, we decided to formulate another plan of action.

Taking a bus from our hotel, we went to the taxi area (known as Places Des Cocotiers) in downtown Noumea. We questioned several taxi-cab drivers (some could speak only French, which I speak fluently) to see if we could find a driver around sixty years of age who could remember the American encampments from World War II. We found most of the men to be in their thirties or forties—too young to remember the early forties when Noumea had a population of only 12,000 people.

At the Tourist Bureau we met a woman who informed us that she knew Daly and would be glad to walk to his office and introduce us. Upon arrival, he very graciously invited us into his private office.

We informed him that LeRoy had been there with the 454th Amphibious Truck Company from September 1943 until January 1944. He told us that he had been with the New Caledonia Army, but had been attached to the Americans for training. He informed us that many companies came in for a short time and then moved out; therefore, he could not recollect the 454th or where they may have been located. However, he did know where all the American camps had been—the general area—and if we had the time, he would be glad to take us around for an hour or more.

Time? The question was, could he spare the time from his official work? He generously advised us that it would be his pleasure. He had written a published article about experiences in New Caledonia during World War II. However, the book is no longer available since the building where it had been kept had burned. Nevertheless, he assured me that he had his copy. He also told us that he is in the process of writing a book, which he really hasn't gotten into fully yet, concerning the New Caledonia allies in the war: the Australians, New Zealanders, and Americans.

We then proceeded with him to the company garage, where he invited us into his French car, and we were off! Incidentally, Daly spoke both French and English, and since I also speak French, it became our primary language of communication.

As we drove through town, he showed us that the present CGM building is located where Admiral Halsey's headquarters had been for a short time; where Menard Freres is located, two blocks further, was the PX during the war. The quonset huts we passed, which now have businesses located in them, were used for storage. These were all located two blocks from the oceanfront.

Opposite the French Colonial Hospital we saw the COMSOPAC (Commander of South Pacific) headquarters, which had been occupied previously by the French army quartermaster. Daly pointed out that in the opposite block, a small one-hundred-bed U.S. hospital named Panettiere Hospital, staffed by the 109th Station Hospital and after a few weeks by the 101st Medical Regiment, had been opened in two girls' orphanages the day after the arrival of Force 6814.

As we drove down the street we could see Nickel Dock in front of us—it was one of the places that LeRoy vividly remembered; we were most thankful to have finally been able to locate it. That was the place that had been blown up by an explosion in November 1943, and the one place from which LeRoy could remember having seen smoke to his left from his encampment.

He could remember that his camp was on a hillside, that they could not see the ocean from it, but that one day when he wandered down to the beach, there had been a lone island in the distance.

Anyone who has traveled to Noumea recently can no longer remember it as it was. There were only 12,000 people there during the war, whereas there are now 70,000. Businesses at that time were very scarce. Where the bus depot now exists used to be the Red Cross Headquarters. (This area was and still remains in a triangle.) In the other triangle, completing the block, was the beer garden where GI entertainment had been— ping-pong, juke boxes, slot machines—for recreation when the servicemen came to town.

Appendix

As we drove, Daly explained that, of course, World War II was in full force in Europe at the time of Pearl Harbor. However, after the Arcadia Conference with England (December 24, 1941–January 14, 1942), the U.S. government had felt that they would concentrate on the Germans and then later on the Japanese.

However, the Australians were concerned about their vulnerability, so it was then decided to send the first expeditionary force, which was the 6814th Division known as the Poppy Force, from New York to New Caledonia. It left New York in January 1942, but did not come straight to New Caledonia, inasmuch as Japanese reconnaissance and American intelligence seemed to think that the Japanese were prepared for the New Caledonia arrival. Therefore, the Poppy Force changed its route and arrived in Melbourne the latter part of February 1942. When they found out that leads had been misinformed, the force then left on March 6 and arrived in Noumea a week later on March 12, 1942. This was the beginning of the Americans on New Caledonia. By February 1943 the island had become a major base for the protection of the South Pacific.

On our way to Dumbea we passed sites of the ABCD (Advance Base Construction Depot) and the NAD (Naval Ammunition Depot). Daly explained that it took twenty-eight days to travel from San Francisco to Noumea by boat and that there were only two cranes at the Nickel Dock (so named because it was, and still is, the dock for the Nickel Company of France). Oftentimes troops would arrive, but many times it took two weeks before the supply ships could be fully unloaded, which created quite a problem.

We then visited the spot where the Eighth General Hospital had been located. It had contained 750 beds. Unbelievable as it was, the two concrete pillars, which had been the entrance to the hospital, were still there. Only three of the ward buildings still remained. They are now used for raising chickens resembling white leghorns. Black asphalt paths throughout the grounds were still visible, although grass has naturally taken over.

Continuing our journey in the Dumbea Valley, we drove to the headquarters of the Twenty-ninth General Hospital, where Daly pointed out that those wards had been made out of prefabricated material. No buildings were left at that site. However, concrete posts with iron rails (which are beginning to corrode), leading up a number of stairs to where the doctors' quarters had been located, were still there. The slab of blacktop, on which the buildings had been built, was also there.

From there we crossed the street and walked through lots of brush (much like blackberry picking at home) and found the slabs where the nurses' quarters had been located. It was a thrill to have come this far and to actually have been able to locate and see signs after thirty-six years. Without Daly we felt our mission would have been impossible, inasmuch as most of the people in the area were about seven or eight years old during World War II.

Below the hospital grounds were dirt roads, but they were still very accessible. Where the hospital supply depot had been, a large quonset hut still stood as evidence, although the metal was obviously rusting. We passed an old rum plant building not too far from the quonset hut.

On the way back to town, Daly reminisced about the songs that were popular in those days—two of which he vividly remembered as "In the Mood" and "El Rancho Grande." Americans must have been singing those tunes over and over again for him to have remembered them so well.

During our trip, Daly stated that at one time there had been 120 ships in the harbor—that the *Lexington, Enterprise,* and *Wasp* had all been there. A net had been installed in the harbor between two points for submarines, and a Navy ship was stationed at the end of the reef to remove the net when our boats and the merchant marine ships had to go through.

In Noumea, he took us to where Major General Vogel had had his headquarters in 1943. The building was white with large white posts and arches (much like a southern mansion) and located on a street corner. He turned the corner and stopped at the back of the building. He told us that Major General Barrett had been delegated to oversee the invasion of Bougainville. Pointing to a window, he informed us that ten days before that invasion, Barrett fell out that window and was killed.

This episode left the Americans frantic, inasmuch as ten days before an invasion it is hard to brief someone new. After great consultations with the higher echelon, it was decided to call General Vandergrift back from Washington, D.C., to oversee this invasion. Vandergrift had been the general in charge of Guadalcanal and was familiar with the area. Thus this was done.

Our trip with Daly was a memorable one—he was so well informed and allowed us to see so much (even where the American cemetery had been during the war; the site is now a New Caledonia cemetery). This was a very impressive and satisfactory first step of our mission through the war zones.

He offered to take us on another drive the next day, but we felt that he had been so generous with his time and information that we should not take further advantage of him. The end of our day came at 10 P.M. We had worked hard but had accomplished something—we felt much gratitude for Daly's helpfulness.

Downtown on Saturday, March 24, 1979, our first stop was the tourist bureau to get information on how to get to various places by bus. They told us that bus number eight would take us out to the American cemetery and that the Paita bus would take us to Tonghoue, which we wanted to revisit.

The cemetery had been built on a hillside. The cement posts and fence built by the Americans still remained, but there were no longer any American graves, since the men had been sent back to the States. Most of the graves in this New Caledonia cemetery are recent, dating from 1973 to 1979, although we did spot one that was marked 1956.

At the top of the hill was the three-tiered podium where the American flag had once flown. The base of the flagstaff with the number 151 on the south side looked like it must have been imbedded in the cement when it was installed, since all evidence proved that this was the original poured concrete—it was beginning to chip.

After thoroughly studying the countryside from this high point, we could see the cone-shaped mountain we had set as a guide sign the day before on our trip via Tonghoue—the ridges in the foreground were where the Army encampments had been.

We spent an hour at the cemetery, and then got our bus back to town. In Noumea we visited the quonset hut area. Some were very rusty but all seemed to be in use. Along the waterfront were square corrugated metal buildings, but the ones a block or two behind were the huts. They had been erected on cement foundations—steel reinforced, but some of the screws connecting the corrugated sheets had fallen out. It was obvious that all had been erected by the Americans and were still standing in their original spots.

We asked some men what the large cement wall west of the hospital had been and which part of the hospital had been erected on it. They informed us it had been built by the Americans and had been the ammunition depot, with the wall continuing underground. It was a slanting wall, still very sturdy, and standing as originally constructed.

Completing our downtown mission, we then returned to our hotel to write up the notes we had made the day before.

On Sunday morning, March 25, we decided to take off by foot to find the motor pool. We had been told it was located near a ridge not too far from our hotel.

As we stood on someone's stairway to admire the many new homes that had been erected on one of the hills, LeRoy spotted a man coming out of his house across the street. French started flying between us and a very informative conversation resulted.

He had spent two years on Wallis Island during the war. He informed us that he had known Halsey very well, and that his aide had gone hunting with him many times on property he owned in the country.

We asked him about the American camps during the war, and he told us that there had been a few along the ocean coast, but a fair number of them had been in the Dumbea area. I told him about our visit with Henri Daly, and he too agreed that he was very knowledgeable.

This gentleman related how the people had been scared to death when, one night, eight battleships came into Noumea. For a day, the people were in a turmoil, thinking the Japanese had arrived, only later to be relieved to find out that the first Americans had arrived. I told him that no doubt it was Force 6814, which had arrived from Melbourne the beginning of March 1943, and that seemed to agree with his thinking.

He told us how the local residents had been able to buy socks, sheets, food, ice cream, and candy at the American PX. The Americans had been very good and would permit the New Caledonians (if accompanied by an American) to buy any goods that were there, which made the people very happy. (I couldn't help but reflect that if the cost of living was then what it is now, it must have been a blessing in disguise to be permitted to get things at GI cost.)

From his home he directed us in the general direction of the motor pool. We walked about one mile in the direction we thought we had been informed to follow. It was a very hot day and the country was very hilly. Along came bus number six; we recognized the bus driver as being the one in whose minibus we had ridden to and from town during the past three days. We stopped him to ask about the motor pool; to make them understand in French you must say "mouter poule."

"Ah, oui," he replied. "Venez avec moi" (Come with me).

We boarded the bus, grateful to get relief from the hot sun. We rode past the area we had walked earlier in the morning, and finally he stopped and said in a French-accented English, "Walk that way, to the right, and you will find it."

No charge for the ride—it was his treat. We had given him our card the previous day and he knew why we were in Noumea!

After walking about three blocks we spotted some old Army equipment and an old tank on tracks in the brush. However, after looking the equipment over, we found that it had not been American.

Continuing our course, we could see Army trucks in the distance. We soon arrived at a place called Gendarmerie Nationale, Caserne Pellisou. It was the headquarters of the French National Guard, where there was a gate and a guard on duty. Speaking in French, I told him why we were there.

He invited us into the grounds and informed us that the large center building, which was a residence hall for the men stationed there, had been built by the Americans. Subsequently, the American plumbing had been replaced with local plumbing. The guard was from France and was serving a three-year period of compulsory military training in New Caledonia. There were large apartment buildings further down the road which were occupied by the servicemen's families.

He then suggested we walk to the top of the hill, which could be seen in the distance. There were still slabs of concrete where the Americans had been camped, he advised, even though brush had taken over the area. I asked him where Nickel Dock was from that point, whereupon he informed us that it was straight ahead but possibly a little to the left.

Arriving at the top, and seeing the large area on the other side, we felt that this had to be the area where the 454th had been camped.

We again passed the guard, thanked him for his help, and continued back to our hotel after four hours of research. We typed up our day's activities and felt that we had completed all the research work in Noumea.

Later that afternoon we walked to the beach and relaxed by visiting with the New Caledonians, who were enjoying their Sunday afternoon with their families. There were lots of sailboats and many swimmers, in addition to those enjoying the warmth of the sun and the clear blue waters of the Anse Vata beach. Incidentally, we were told that there were 8,000 pleasure boats in Noumea.

The city of Noumea is very beautiful and well laid out, with three wonderful beaches located within minutes of the city center. It is located close to the southern tip of the island of New Caledonia, which is approximately 400 kilometers long and 50 kilometers wide.

The bus service, consisting mostly of minibuses, is excellent. The people are very friendly and helpful, and they do enjoy visiting with Americans. A loaf of French bread, fruit, and wine make a terrific cassecroute (snack)!

New Hebrides

Early Monday morning, March 26, we took the airport bus to Tontouta, where we were to catch our flight for Porta Vila, New Hebrides. I won't go into details concerning our visa problem at the airport, but we do want to suggest that if any of our readers intend to visit New Hebrides, be sure that the French Consulate, which issues the visa, distinctly marks it "Valable pour les Nouvelle Hebrides." A French visa that doesn't state this will not be accepted.

We spent Monday through Friday in Port Vila, inasmuch as we discovered prior to leaving the United States that many of the smaller islands do not have flights every day and some only have flights to specific areas. Our next stop was to be Honiara, Guadalcanal, so we had to wait until Friday for that flight.

Nevertheless, we enjoyed our four-day stay in the New Hebrides very much. This country has a condominium government and is ruled by both the French and British. A tour of the city took us to the French quarters and the British quarters of Vila, where each has its own hospital, city hall, and other separate institutions. However, both the French flag and the British flag fly on all buildings and at the same height—no discrimination!

Our hotel was about one and a half miles out of town, but the bus service (twenty cents each way) was very good. We met two New Zealand travel agents who were staying at the hotel who taught us an easy way to convert Celsius to Fahrenheit—just multiply the Celsius degrees times two and add thirty. Another thing they taught us was to take the last figure off of kilometers and multiply by six—to give you the approximate number of miles. We, American travelers, learned something from the New Zealanders, in addition to the fact that they are very friendly people and enjoy describing their beautiful country.

Our last day at Port Vila was LeRoy's sixty-fifth birthday. It was hard to believe that on March 30, 1944, thirty-five years before, he had spent his birthday on Guadalcanal—where we would be arriving the next day!

Guadalcanal

Needless to say, we were very excited Saturday morning as we boarded our flight to Honiara, Guadalcanal. In a short time we were to be on the first island where LeRoy had spent a considerable amount of time driving DUKWs, and from which he was subsequently transferred to the island of Pavuvu to train for combat with the First Marine Division.

We arrived at Henderson Field around 10:30 A.M. and took the bus to our hotel, located one short block from the main downtown area of Honiara. After checking into our room, our first course of action was to drink to the 454th Amphibious Truck Company and all the Army buddies.

Located across the street from our hotel was the Honiara Museum, where we found substantial information and pamphlets on the Guadalcanal campaign. West of our hotel we found a monument erected in memory of World War II soldiers. The plaque on the front read, "In commemoration of the Liberation of the Solomon Islands, which began with the landing of the United States Forces on the 7th of August, 1942. This plaque was laid by Honorary Sub Inspector Vouza, MBE, GM on the 7th of August, 1967."

On the right of this tall pillar-type monument was another plaque, which read, "At this spot, on August Seventh 1967, a wreath was laid by representatives of the United States Marine Corps in reverent memory of the sacrifice of the heroic men of all the nations, arms and services who

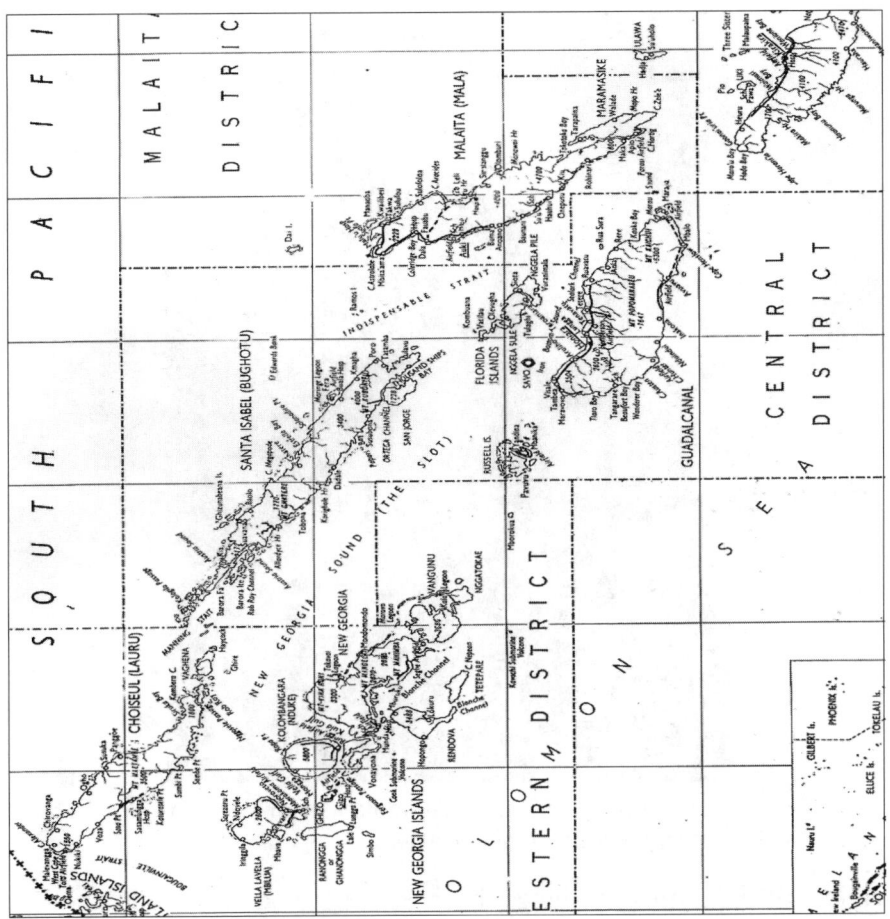

Map of South Pacific

took part in the battle for Guadalcanal and the Liberation of the Solomons a quarter of a century earlier."

Sunday, April 1 (April Fool's Day), immediately reminded us of the invasion of Okinawa, as that was D-Day there in 1945. We decided that since Sunday is usually a quiet day, we would investigate the downtown area of Honiara. Some of the little shops along the way were open until noon, and many natives were taking advantage of this.

We walked through every one of the shops, but found that they were all basically the same. Most were operated by Chinese who arrived there in the early 1960s. They had a little bit of everything in the stores—

155

Monument in Honiara, Guadalcanal erected in memory of World War II Soldiers

children's and adults' clothing, shoes, canned goods (in small amounts and varieties), and even bread.

We noticed some quonset huts being used by the Solomon Island government, located right along the ocean shore. Exploring a field, we found some pontoons that had been there during the war and were heavily corroded. These were located just before the one-lane bridge that crosses the Matanikau River. Crossing the bridge, we found that we were in Chinatown, and proceeded to walk through several of the stores, which were all similar to the ones we had previously seen.

Throughout all our travels that day LeRoy was busy autographing our cards, which we were handing out concerning our book. In addition he showed his sleight-of-hand tricks. It was amusing to see the faces of the same natives, several blocks further on, who had run to catch up with us and wanted him to show the magic to their friends. They all seemed very interested in the book, and we thoroughly enjoyed mingling and visiting with these natives.

Since it was Sunday, the two weekly boats at Point Cruz (the local dock) were loading passengers—one ship was going to Bougainville and the other to Savo Island. There were many natives at the pier seeing their friends and relatives off for the outer islands. It was a festive atmosphere, with lots of soda and beer consumed, as humidity was very high as well as the temperature.

April 2 found us eager to start our work. After contacting a local travel office in the hopes of being able to take a tour of the World War II battlefields, we were told we would have to wait until 8:30 A.M. the following day.

Rather than waste the day, we decided to take a cab and do some exploring on our own. Since LeRoy had been camped in the direction of Henderson Field, we asked a cabdriver what he would charge to take us there. When he told us four dollars, we decided to bargain for an hourly price. At five dollars per hour, we were on our way!

We approached Henderson Field from the west and went to the end of the strip, only to find that there was no road going south. Continuing on the main blacktop road for about another mile, we found a coral road and took it. Driving parallel to the airfield, we could see this was not the place we were looking for, since there were no coconut trees.

In the distance, across the airstrip, we could see groves of coconut trees, however, and our driver informed us that there was a coral road on the other side of the main highway.

We drove back toward the Lungga River and in a short time found the road we were looking for. LeRoy felt that this was the area and kept looking for a road that would take off toward the ocean, as he could remember there being a "T" where he was camped. After driving only a mile and a half, the bottom "T" was spotted. When we arrived at that point he was sure that the post office had been located on the northwest corner, and that his 454th had been located on the northeast corner. We spotted two men walking up the road toward us as we arrived at the "T," so LeRoy asked them if there had been camps here during the war. They said there had, so from then on we were on the right track; we had arrived!

The older of the two men, fifty-seven years of age, told us he had worked with the Americans for about three years during the war; they had nicknamed him Spy and he was mighty proud of his name. He was originally from Malaita Island, a short distance from Guadalcanal, and was now working for the Lever copra plantation. The other gentleman with him worked for the same company, and we later found out that Spy was the boss on this particular plantation.

He told us that he could show us many places in the area, and he and his friend agreed to go along with us in our taxi. First, we examined the grounds at the start of the "T." We noticed that the gate on the left was still where the post office had been. Then we examined the grounds on the right of the entrance of this road, and walked a short distance down it to the point where the DUKW drivers would drive their vehicles into the campground area. Behold, there were several steel grated sections for road beds cast in the ditch where DUKWs once turned into camp.

Entrance to 454th Amphibious Truck Company campground, Guadalcanal, April 2, 1979

From there we drove east to a point where the American cemetery used to be; the flagpole was still there, and there was the low grass field in front of it, a reminder of the American graves that had been there. However, all bodies were removed for burial on American soil after the war. One lonely orange flower, resembling a poppy, and no doubt the sole remaining plant originally planted in the cemetery, was still blooming in the center of the area after thirty-six years.

Spy then asked if we wanted to go to the dump, which we did. We went through a plantation gate and down the road, which had originally been built by the GIs. At the dump were acres of corroded vehicles and machinery, but there was no DUKW. Cattle were grazing along the ocean to the left of it as we proceeded along the grassy, weed-covered old GI road, and we found an abandoned alligator with its tracks still on it!

While traveling this road I thought I had spotted the bottom ridges of an amphibious DUKW in the brush, so from the alligator we retraced our journey while I kept my eyes peeled in the hopes of again spotting it. When I finally did, the car stopped, and both of us ran. It was a DUKW—

Ground where American cemetery used to be on Guadalcanal. Note the flagpole in the center background and the lone poppy blooming in the foreground.

what a thrill! It was like old home week—not only finding the original campground, but also being fortunate enough to locate a DUKW, even though it was upside down and the front end had corroded away. Nevertheless the rudder was still very much in sight, as well as the complete rear of the vehicle.

As I maneuvered through other forms of metal and debris to take a picture, about ten feet from the DUKW I spotted a steering wheel. LeRoy removed some of the ivy that was growing on the vehicle and then posed holding the steering wheel. It would have been great to take the steering wheel home with us, but we were only starting our journey and we had a long way to travel.

From there we returned to where the 454th had camped. Our two guides departed to return to their work, but LeRoy and I just could not leave the spot. I took pictures of the terrain from various points, so that we would have a remembrance of the whole area. We noticed that many of the coconut trees had been cut, and that there was quite a bit of brush lying around. The ground is owned by the Lungga Lever Plantation, the local copra company—copra being the main industry on Guadalcanal.

Typical road built by the G.I.s in 1942 after the invasion of Guadalcanal, and how it looks thirty-six years later.

We continued to the end of the road, which led to the ocean—the spot where the DUKWs came onto the beach when they hauled cargo from the ships anchored offshore. On the right, facing the ocean, was a copra sacking plant where six or seven natives were working.

Retracing our trip back, passing the 454th camp on the left, we turned at the "T" to start our return trip into Honiara. On the road we again found our two guides, who had decided to walk toward their work crew. Where they were standing was where the Island Command and USO had been. The field is now overgrown with grass, weeds, and brush.

Spy then had his workers get two coconuts so that we could have coconut milk, while LeRoy showed them some of his coin tricks. We then proceeded back to Honiara, crossing the Lungga River one-lane bridge along the way.

On our return to the hotel, the cabdriver told us we owed him fifteen dollars. We would gladly have paid him as much as he wanted because of the success we had had.

It had been a very warm, humid day on Guadalcanal. We did a lot of sweating, and LeRoy remarked several times that that was the way it had been when he was there back in early 1944. That night, as he sat on our

Rear end of DUKW found on Guadalcanal, April 2, 1979. Note rudder is plainly vissible in center of picture.

161

Same DUKW as in previous Illustration, but this photograph was taken from the side. Front end of vehicle had corroded, and ivy, which had to be removed, fully covered the vehicle. Steering wheel in LeRoy's hand was found in brush.

lanai writing some thoughts in poetry, there was the roaring of the ocean and trees were whipping back and forth—the beginnings of a tropical storm.

It had been quite an emotional day for us—a great joy in being able to locate the spot where LeRoy had been with the 454th, and yet moments of sadness finding us both with tears trickling down our cheeks several times. April 2, 1979, will always live in our memories.

Trip to World War II Battlefields

At 8:30 A.M. Tuesday, April 3, we started with our guide to tour the battlefields of World War II. We went east toward Henderson Field on the only road going in that direction. (It is paved to the east of Henderson Field only; beyond that it is coral.)

Road leading to Lungga Beach, Guadalcanal. The 454th Amphibious Truck Company camp site had been in the coconut grove on the right side.

Our first stop was at what was known during wartime as Sun Valley. It has since been taken over by a church group. On the road into their carving and display center, we passed the site where large amounts of used and unused American equipment from trucks, jeeps, and ammunition were buried at the end of the war.

Over this dump, which lies between two hillsides, natives had planted vegetation and edible foods. We were told that systematic salvaging of this site for scrap metal provides a source of income for a mission high school, which now occupies this valley. We stopped at the carving showroom and workshop to see the hand-carved masks, bowls, and war clubs, which are all inlaid with mother-of-pearl. The wood is beautiful and each item is expertly made.

On the outside of the building were remains of airplanes (parts of them) that either crashed, burned, or were shot down in the war. It appeared that most of those on display were Japanese Zero fighters.

Appendix

We then returned to the main highway, then crossed the Lungga River bridge and stopped to see the foxhole of Colonel Fox. He was commander of the forces at Henderson during World War II. We were able to walk into the concrete foxhole, which was built in the hillside and consisted of a large room with an entryway and also a hole for light.

We visited the underground hospital, built for emergency purposes only, which was a short distance from there. Oxygen gas had been supplied to the interior during the occupation period. It consisted of four rooms. Holes remained where posts could have been installed to support beams to hold up the roof (called cribbing in mines).

Retracing part of our journey, we then took the road to Bloody Ridge, also known as Edson's Ridge. Along the way, we crossed a bunker for the storage of guns, and in a short time arrived at the top of the ridge. There was erected a three-sided, sharp-pointed monument, which had a plaque of copper embedded in the cement, reading, "During the six months' battle for Guadalcanal from 7 Aug. 1942 to 9 Feb. 1943, the battle for 'Edson's Ridge' stands out as one of the most fiercely contested engagements between U.S. Marines and Japanese forces. During 12–13 Sept. the Japanese

Foxhole of Colonel Fox, commander of forces at Henderson Field, Guadalcanal, during World War II.

launched a determined counterattack from the jungle south and east of this hill against Marine raider and parachute troops commanded by Col. Merritt A. Edson as the first phase in a coordinated offensive to recapture Henderson Field. After two nights of savage fighting, the Japanese under the command of Major General Kiyotake Kawaguchi were defeated with severe casualties, and never seriously threatened the airfield again. This monument stands in the area in which Colonel Edson's men rallied and repulsed the last enemy attacks."

Official maps show that the Japanese attacked from the south and east. It must have been a real jungle from the looks of it today. The Americans, however, had a high ridge on which to maintain their position and successfully defeat the Japanese attack. This was the Japanese's last effort to retake Henderson Field, which the Americans had previously captured from them. We took a lower road under Bloody Ridge, which is now overgrown with brush, in order to get a better view of the ridge itself.

Our next stop was the control tower at the west end of Henderson Field, which is no longer in use since a new one has been erected at the

Monument on top of Bloody Ridge (also known as Edson's Ridge) Guadalcanal, commemorating the fierce battle between U.S. Marines and Japanese Forces in September, 1942.

terminal located halfway down the runway. The old tower was erected by the Americans to replace the Japanese one. (Henderson Field, incidentally, was named after Major Lofton Henderson, Marine hero of the Midway Island campaign.)

We decided to climb the seventy-foot tower even though some of the wooden steps have rotted away, leaving only the metal reinforcements, about five to six inches wide. There were a total of five rows of stairs to the top, beginning with twelve at the bottom, then a platform, then twelve to the left, fifteen more, then fourteen, with the final ten to the top, where there was a large wooden platform.

Old control tower at Henderson Field, Guadalcanal built by U.S. Air Force Engineers in June 1942, which still stands at the west end of the airfield.

From this high point we could once again see the coconut grove area of the 454th encampment. It was easy to distinguish because of the metal roof, which is on a shack north of where the company was camped. This shack is actually one-half of a quonset hut in which natives now live.

At the foot of this control tower was a wooden sign, which read, "CONTROL TOWER HENDERSON FIELD built by United States Air Force Engineers June 1942. Rehabilitated by Public Works Department November 1969."

From there we proceeded across Alligator Creek, where Hell's Point is located. This is where collected bombs were disposed of after the war. We soon arrived at Red Beach, which was where Allied forces, on August

Red Beach where Allied Forces landed on August 7, 1942 on D-Day, Guadalcanal. Note old piling used for the war remains.

7, 1942, landed under cover of fire from naval ships, and immediately advanced west and south. We were told that by 8 P.M. the same night, 10,000 Allies (mainly Marines) had landed on Guadalcanal—this was the first landing!

From the beach we could see Ironbottom Sound, the stretch of water between the Island of Guadalcanal and the Island of Savo, so named because of the number of both American and Japanese ships sunk in those waters. The Battle of Savo, as it was called, is considered to have been the worst defeat in the history of the American Navy.

Retracing back to the main highway, we crossed the Tenaru River, where there was a one-way bridge. However, still visible, resting in water to the north of this bridge crossing, was the old rusted American bridge that was built when our troops were there.

Crossing the Ngalimbiu River and driving through the town of Ngalimbiu, we turned in the direction of Koli Point. This was where LeRoy had been hurt when stationed here. The five miles of an old GI road, no longer used, had been taken over by high grass and brush. Nevertheless, our driver moved right along, hitting bumps at a pretty fast speed. Sometimes the chuckholes were filled with water from the rain we had had during the night, and at times the muddy water splashed into the car. This did not faze our guide, however. He certainly went out of his way to

Looking east along Red Beach, Guadalcanal. This four-mile long beach is where U.S. Marines landed on August 7, 1942.

take us wherever we asked, and wherever he thought we might be interested in going.

On our way back to Honiara, but just before reaching Henderson Airfield, our driver took a coral road to the north, and in a short time we were back once again at the 454th camp area, which pleased us very much. It seemed for three days our paths always led us to that spot!

Later that day we tried to get reservations to fly to Pavuvu, where the 454th had trained before the invasion of Peleliu. We discovered that the planes went only three times a week to Yandina on Banika Island, that Copra Plantation Company owned the island of Pavuvu, and that the only way to get to it was by their barge from Yandina. However, we did find out that it was a one-hour boat ride each way. With the airline schedule we would have had only an hour on the island, so we decided we had better not chance the trip.

Wednesday, April 4, proved to be cloudy and showery, so we decided we would spend the day writing. Mosquitoes were beginning to really have a feast on me, so I welcomed the day in the hotel.

Remains of American bridge built across the Tenaru River, Guadalcanal in 1942. New concrete bridge, crossing the river can be seen on the right side.

Koli Point, Guadalcanal as seen on April 2, 1979. This is the site where the 454th Amphibious Truck Company hauled supplies from ships to shore for stockpiling; here too the First Marine Division was loaded for their Pavuvu training.

Our Trip to the Tetere Area

We decided on April 5 to take a glass-bottomed boat from our hotel dock for a two-and-a-half-hour ride on the ocean around Point Cruz. We were able to see an American F4F Wildcat fighter, a relic of World War II, sitting in thirty-two feet of clear water; a tank with only the top visible could also be seen. We passed the mouth of the Matanikau River, a famous battle spot alongside of which is now Honiara's Chinatown.

During the trip we met a missionary from California who had been on Guadalcanal for several months. He told us that he was using Sergeant Major Jacob Vouza's car (which carries the U.S. Marine Corps emblem on the side of the door). When we informed him that we had wanted to visit Vouza, he suggested that we follow him back home that afternoon.

At 3 P.M. we rendezvoused in front of the hotel, hired a taxi, and were on our way to the Tetere area, where Vouza lived. We went along our usual route, traveling east of town, which was via Henderson Airfield, Alligator Creek, Tenaru River, and Ngalimbiu River. (We really began to get oriented since we had traveled the area every day, and our native drivers were amazed at two Americans on Guadalcanal who knew where they were going!)

After going through the town of Ngalimbiu and crossing the Matepono River, we passed the Solomon Island Oil Palm Plantation processing plant, and continued through palm trees and rice fields to a second processing plant where we left the main highway. After traveling a short distance, we arrived at a Melanesian village. On the right side of the road was the local church, and next to it was Vouza's home. He and his wife Irene were there, as well as their daughter and her family.

Vouza, a native Guadalcanalian, was very glad to see us. He very graciously posed for a picture with LeRoy and then for one with his wife. We so very much enjoyed visiting with him and his family. He told us that he had been invited to the United States and to many worldwide functions throughout the years, including Queen Elizabeth's inauguration. He was so appreciative of all these courtesies extended to him.

He had helped our armed forces greatly in their struggle to secure the island. Yet he was so humble and so thankful to have been able to do his part, and so grateful for the honors bestowed upon him. Since our visit he has been knighted by the Queen of England. He is a great man.

Alongside the church was a little garden enclosed with a picket fence, in which there was a monument presented to him by the U.S. Marine Raiders Association. The bronze plaque on the memorial read, "We dedicate to Sergeant Major Jacob Vouza and his Solomon Island Scouts for supreme intrepidity and valour in the face of the enemy during the struggle for Guadalcanal 1942–43. Presented by the Marine Raiders Association."

He had a portion of his tongue cut off and was bayoneted twice in his chest by a Japanese naval officer. Nevertheless, he refused medical attention until he had given the U.S. forces a full report on the strength and location of the enemy.

Appendix

LeRoy gave him an autographed card, a small gesture of appreciation for his time. We bade him farewell as I kissed each of his cheeks, which he seemed to enjoy. As we got into our taxi, he blessed us with a saying that went something like this—"May God bless you and be with you as you travel on your journey, and may he bless those whom we were associated with during the war." He then shook each of our hands, wished us well, and told us to go with Godspeed.

Vouza had informed our driver where we could find some amphibious vehicles: near mango trees, beyond the second plantation plant. We found two amtracs alongside the road, and continued past the many trees in the hopes of finding more vehicles in the brush. Along came a pedestrian who worked for the plantation, and who informed us that he knew where there were some vehicles. We walked along the ocean road and then turned into a field full of brush and high grass. We found two more amtracs side by side, and further down the road we discovered two more that were pretty well covered. We were disappointed in not finding any DUKWs, but were happy to have found what we had.

Sergeant Major Jacob Vouza and LeRoy on April 2, 1979. Taken in front of his home in Tetere Area of Guadalcanal.

Driving back to Honiara, we were amazed at the modern farm machinery that they had out in the country. We saw large combines working the rice fields, and the farmers apparently worked the same long hours as ours do in the States, since they were still working the combines at dusk.

Friday, April 6, we were up at daybreak typing all the pages of the story that had been written the night before. However, by 10:30 A.M. we had hired a cab and were on our way to Visale, about twenty miles from Honiara and at the northwestern tip of the island, to visit a war museum. Along the way we stopped just east of the Ponaki River and walked to the beach where we saw the remains of a Japanese ship that had been left there during the war. Most of it was sunken into the ocean, but we could see the bow and aft protruding high in the air.

At the war museum, the owner was not there but his wife and family were present. After paying the entrance fee, we were taken through the customary houses, which are typical of the Solomon Islands and other islands we have visited; we then walked through the beautifully kept tropical

Sergeant Major Jacob Vouza and his wife pose on Guadalcanal in front of monument presented to him and his Solomon Island Scouts by the U.S. Marine Raiders Association.

173

gardens. We saw a small crocodile, which they had in captivity and were raising for food—apparently they eat the tails as a delicacy.

Finally we reached the spot we had really come to see. That location revealed the planes, guns, and other machinery that had been collected throughout the island as remnants of World War II. There was a U.S. Corsair, an F4F Wildcat that had been on the U.S.S. *Hornet* aircraft carrier (but was still in fairly good condition, considering it had crashed) and finally, the remnants of the wings of a plane they told us had come from the U.S.S. *Saratoga.* There were also several large artillery guns that had been restored, which were of Japanese vintage. We then entered a thatched-roof building in which were displayed Japanese helmets, machine guns, and rifles to the left, and American ones that had been found and oiled up for preservation to the right.

Upon our return to the hotel we continued our book work and then started packing for our onward trip to Papua New Guinea the next day. Our next port of call, so to speak, was to be New Guinea because that was the route we had to take to finally get to Peleliu. Our route called for New

Two abandoned Amtracs found under a tree in the bush country of the Tetere Area, Guadalcanal. Several more of these vehicles were found in the same area.

Guinea, the Philippines, Guam, and then Peleliu. (The only way by air to get to the Palau Islands, of which Peleliu is one, is via Guam.)

By noon Saturday, April 7, we were on our way to Henderson Airfield, also known as Honiara International Airport. We took one last look at the 454th Amphibious Truck Company's campsite, which we had pegged by now as being across from the old control tower (the one we had walked up earlier in the week).

Truthfully, we both hated to leave Guadalcanal. It had many memories for the both of us, and assuming that this was probably the last time we would be there, it was kind of like losing a friend. We had been so fortunate in finding the place of encampment, so fortunate in finding Spy to show us around, and so lucky to find Lungga Point, Red Beach, and Koli Point. The natives had been so good to us and so very helpful, and it had been indeed an honor and privilege for us to meet Vouza and his family. This was Guadalcanal, a place that LeRoy will never forget as it was in 1943–44, and a place we both will never forget as it was in 1979.

New Guinea

Our flight from Honiara to Kieta, New Guinea, took fifty-five minutes. Once there, we had to disembark to have our international medical cards checked for smallpox and cholera. After getting our New Guinea visas stamped with the date of entry, we again boarded the plane for our one-and-a-half-hour flight to Port Moresby.

Entering Port Moresby was the simplest formality of any entry we had had so far. We merely showed our passports and our disembarkation forms, and gathered up our suitcases. Going through customs consisted merely of the agent picking up the form we had filled out regarding food, meats, and the like, and that was it.

However, we quickly found out that we were only getting sixty-three cents on our American dollar—this was going to hurt! Our hotel was quite comfortable but a distance out of town. When we arrived in our room, the first thing we noticed was a sign informing us to be sure to bolt our door at night, as they found robberies happened in the night when the bolt was not on. We had been told by a gentleman on the flight to Port

Moresby, who had been there before, that it wasn't safe to walk alone in the streets at night and that it wasn't safe for a woman to walk alone anytime. Nevertheless we never had any trouble all the time we were there.

Sunday morning we walked into town. Although all the stores were closed, we familiarized ourselves with the surroundings and found a new hotel right on the hill overlooking the bay.

We rode a local bus to the end of its line. (We had checked with our driver when we boarded the bus to make sure he would bring us back to the boarding spot and that he was going to make the round trip.)

The countryside was very beautiful but we couldn't help but notice how poor the people were. There were markets in various towns along the way. Lots of bananas and greens were for sale. Many people came on the bus with their purchases—one little boy had two strings of fish with him. Most of the women had two or three children with them, ranging from six months to three years of age, or else (as the Australian expression we learned on our trip put it) they had a "bun in the oven."

We did notice, however, that all the men were very good to the small children. More times than not, they would be the ones carrying the small children in their arms. Mothers nursed the babies right on the bus, on the street, or wherever and whenever the need arose.

Almost everyone was barefoot—a practice I learned immediately when we arrived in the South Pacific! The people are clean looking—they wear clean clothes, and in spite of the hot climate there is no body odor. They are darker in color than the Polynesians, although as we rode the bus, I found out that my tan was darker than the color of the woman sitting next to me.

Monday was spent moving, exchanging U.S. money for kinas and toyas, and reconfirming our onward flight to Guam via Manila.

During the next few days we took an all-day bus tour to the Owen Stanley Ranges, went along the Kokoda Trail (where there is a monument erected for men who fought the Japanese on that ridge in 1942), and saw how they tap rubber trees and have cups collecting the rubber fluid, which they then pour into gallon pails.

We also enjoyed going to Waigini to visit the National Museum, which opened in 1977. On display were lots of face masks, shields, drums used for hauling water, full figures of men and women (some looked like petrified wood), and lots of beautiful carvings. One room contained charts on health, showing the causes and remedies for such things as gonorrhea, syphilis, TB, cholera, and malaria. There were also charts on birth control.

After spending five enjoyable days in Port Moresby, we bade New Guinea farewell on Friday, April 13. We were on our way to Guam, with a stopover in Manila merely to change planes. Our arrival in Guam was quite late as we went through U.S. customs. We had to give up a pandanus fan that had been made and given to us by our maid at our hotel in Port Vila, New Hebrides—no coconut leaves of any kind could be brought in.

We enjoyed our one-and-a-half-day stay on Guam. It was somewhat of a preliminary recognizance, since we knew we would be returning there to get to Okinawa. We decided to leave one of our suitcases at the hotel, since we were finding that two suitcases, a typewriter, and and attaché case were too much to carry around. This called for a morning's repacking, after which we walked into the town of Agana to visit the stores and shops.

Easter Sunday, April 15, 1979, we walked along the beach in front of our hotel and discovered what was once a pillbox used by the Japanese during the war. After a hearty brunch we headed for the airport and our one-hour-and-forty-five-minute flight to Koror. The runway at Palau International Airport at Airai on Babelthuap (pronounced and spelled by natives as Babeldaob) didn't seem very long as we landed. We just made it for the turnaround as the field ended. A fire truck was stationed along the runway, and we later found out that it came from town whenever a plane was scheduled to arrive.

The plane unloaded and immediately reloaded for the flight back to Guam. The airport was very small—only one counter in the open; that must have been because the temperature was warm. Passengers could check their luggage and their tickets, and get a Coke or 7-UP all at the same counter. Hand baggage was checked by one girl at the gate as you boarded. The checked luggage was hand-carried off the plane, put on large trucks, and then handed over a high fence and put on the rack for individual pickup. You then went through customs; in our case they just OKed and waved us through. The toilet consisted of an outhouse.

It was a twenty-minute bus ride to our hotel. Many passengers had brought their scuba diving equipment along with them, and so the bus was packed. The hotel was situated on a hillside overlooking the floating rock islands, and the view was spectacular. The island looked like large mounds of trees scattered here and there. Water had washed the rocks around the islands, making them appear as though they were just resting on top of the water. They looked like mushrooms!

Our first detail Monday morning was to make arrangements to go to Peleliu. We had been informed that there was only a boat that made the trip once a day. We were pleasantly surprised to find that a Palau Island commuter plane (Aero Belau) made two trips each day. We were told to be ready at 7:45 A.M. the next day, when we would be picked up by our pilot and taken to the airport. We would then fly to Peleliu, where a pickup with a guide would take us to the Chief of the Island's home, where we were to stay overnight and from which we were to return to Koror the following day.

After those arrangements, we hired a taxi to take us to the Communications Center at Malakal so that we could phone our daughter in the United States. Since the lines were so busy we couldn't get through, we sent a telegram instead.

Our driver told us he would take us around the island if we so desired. We jumped at the opportunity. We visited the Japanese seaplane ramp that had been used during the war, and then drove to the Mitsui Harbour plant, where we could see a Japanese cave up on the hillside. From there we were taken to the fish wharf, where we saw some tuna being brought in—some were fifteen-pounders.

Lunch was eaten at a small restaurant run by Palauans. The menu consisted mostly of Japanese dishes, but our driver ordered oyako domburi for us. It had a rice base with what looked like scrambled eggs, vegetables, and boiled chicken on top. It was delicious topped with Tabasco sauce and soy sauce. In Koror they have Tabasco sauce in the large forty-four, ounce bottle and the natives seem to use it as freely as we do catsup. Being admirers of highly seasoned foods, we found the meal a treat.

The town of Koror does not have too many shops; most are small and privately owned. There were a few nice new cement (or stucco) homes, but most of them were older and made out of corrugated sheet metal, much like workers' homes in other parts of the South Pacific.

We spent two hours at the Palau Museum. The gentleman there is an artist and had some reprints of some of his works on display. Both he and the young lady librarian were most helpful. They had some Peleliu material—several mimeographed War Command resumes of Operation Stalemate, which contained information on the Peleliu invasion as well as of that of Angaur. (Peleliu was September 15, 1944, and Angaur was September 17, 1944.) We saw a picture of a DUKW taken at the time of the invasion of Peleliu, so LeRoy left an autographed card, which they placed next to the picture. He promised that when we returned home he would

PALAU MUSEUM
Hera Ware Owen, Director
Francisco Morei, Chairman

Koror, Palau, Caroline Islands 96940

Date: __21 August 1979__

THE PALAU MUSEUM INCORPORATED

Acknowledges receipt of ___So. Pacific Seashell Cross___

From ___Lilly & LeRoy Bronemann___

Address ___Box B, Fall City, Wash. U.S.A. 98024___

For the purpose of ___(gift) display___

Faustina Rehuher
Faustina Rehuher
PALAU MUSEUM DIRECTOR

The staff and management of the Palau Museum would like to say "thank you" for such a generous gift.

We would like to know more about "Once Upon a Tide". Please keep us in mind.

PALAU MUSEUM
Established in 1955

Non-profit Corporation
Chartered by the Trust Territory of the Pacific Islands.
Saipan, Mariana Islands of the

Communication received from Palau Museum acknowledging receipt of an authentic South Pacific Sea Shell Cross, which LeRoy made and sent to them on our return to the U.S.

make up a South Pacific Cross and send it to the Palau Museum to add to this display. This has been done as evidenced by their acknowledgment.

On the same grounds as the museum was the A-frame Bai (men's meeting place), which we also visited. It was repaired after the 1976 typhoon. Men now meet in their homes, however, since they have air conditioning and more comforts than afforded by the Bai. In the building was a place where they could build fires for cooking, and the beams were wood carved with storybook insignia—very beautiful.

From there we asked our driver to stop at a supermarket, which was very much like ours at home, although perhaps a little smaller. We wanted to purchase groceries to take with us to Peleliu the next day, since we had heard there had been a recent typhoon and subsequent damage there. We thought a few items would be a nice gesture and might be needed by our host and his family.

Peleliu

Neither one of us slept much that night, and Tuesday morning, April 17, 1979, found us waiting in the hotel lobby, long before our scheduled appointment at 7:45. Our pilot, Bob, who arrived in his pickup, was on time; he had already picked up a passenger for the flight. She and I sat in the front seat with Bob, and LeRoy rode in the back of the pickup on the bumpy road to Airai and the Palau International Airport on Babelthuap Island.

Bob and a native helper, who was waiting at the airport, untied the 250 Cessna plane with Bob doing a few checkouts. We then boarded Aero Belau for our fifteen-minute flight to Peleliu from Babelthuap Island, where the airport for Koror is located. Both islands are connected by a bridge and both, as well as Peleliu, are part of the Palau Islands.

I sat on the right side of the plane, as Bob had suggested it was best for pictures. We were also heading south and due to the morning sun, the west side of the plane was the best. The view of the Floating Rock Islands below us was absolutely fantastic; we were flying at approximately twelve hundred feet and the sun was shining in clear blue sky. It was a perfect day to fly! Every island (and there are over three hundred of them) presented a different image. Centuries of water erosion have severely undercut their rocky bases, and it gives one the illusion that someone has just dropped them in certain spots, and that they are floating on top of the water. The early morning sun added to their mystical form, and the ever-changing shapes and shades were really a sight to behold.

We landed on the Peleliu airfield, which was originally built by the Japanese and later taken over by the Americans in the invasion of Peleliu on September 15, 1944. The invasion was to seize the island and thereby neutralize the Japanese supply forces for Manila.

The airstrip was of coral that was really packed down. It was very wide and a little rough in spots where heavy rains had washed out the runway and left chuckholes. There were some weeds and grass shooting up through the coral, but basically it was not a bad landing field for a small plane. The terminal consisted of an open shed made of poles— poles for the roof, poles for the sides, and poles to sit on—all narrow ones about three to four inches around.

Original airstrip built by the Japanese and later taken by the Americans in the invasion of Peleliu, September 15, 1979, on our visit to Peleliu, Palau Islands.

Appendix

Waiting at the airport for us was Reiko—an attractive native woman, who was small in stature and who seemed to be about thirty-five to forty years of age. She had a yellow pickup which had a board across the bed for the passengers to sit on, located at the back of the cab window. She was the local agent for Aero Belau, and the official picker-upper and deliverer for the plane. The plane made two round trips per day—one in the morning at 8:15 and the other leaving Peleliu at 4:45 at night. It went from Koror to Peleliu, then on to Angaur, and returned. (Angaur is a five-minute ride from Peleliu.)

On our morning flight there was only one passenger in addition to us. We did not find out until our arrival on Peleliu, that we had flown with the mother of the Chief of Peleliu. The Chief, called Obak by the natives in due respect although his real name is Isao Singeo, was forty-two years of age. His mother, whose name is Toyomi Singeo and who was sixty-three years of age, is called Balang by the natives. She and her husband, Techung Singeo, lived on Koror.

There was another man in a pickup waiting for the return flight to Koror, and so while our pilot took the five-minute hop to Angaur, that man, Balang, and Reiko visited with us. Balang could not speak English, but Reiko was the interpreter, and she seemed to enjoy the visit. She related how she, her family, and the residents of Peleliu had had leaflets dropped on the island by the Americans instructing them to leave the island, as they were going to bomb and invade it. She told us that most of the people left by boat and went to Babelthuap on their own. However, the Japanese also helped them evacuate by taking some of them by boat over to Babelthuap.

She explained how it felt to have bombs dropping and guns firing, and how scared they all were. She told us that the Americans built them new homes after the war and that some of the people moved back to the island in 1947–49. LeRoy autographed a card for her and she seemed very pleased to receive it.

By then Bob had returned from Angaur and the man had boarded the plane with him. Reiko unloaded the rest of the freight that had been sent, and placed it in the pickup. Balang, another woman who had been waiting near the shed for a ride, LeRoy, and I got into the truck. We headed for town, which was about a five-mile drive, over coral roads that were actually in much better condition than were those on Koror.

Reiko informed us that we could stay with the chief overnight (unbeknownst to him, we were sure). When we arrived at his home we were introduced to him. He was working in his backyard with several other men repairing a bulldozer. Being busy at the time, he didn't seem too impressed with our arrival, but did wipe his hands so he could shake ours. He told his mother and Reiko to take us into the house. It was aqua in color and made of stucco. The inside was very large and most comfortable.

The chief told us to sit and rest and that he would find a guide to take us around the island. He offered us a glass of cold water, as it was a very hot day, and then went about his business. We sat on the sofa for about one-half hour enjoying the coolness of his home. He came in the house several times to assure us that someone would be coming very soon. We did not meet his wife, but did see a young woman helping Balang in the kitchen. We did not know what they were doing, but when our guide arrived to pick us up, Chief Obak informed us that our lunch was ready; the two women had fixed a large picnic basket and a jug of cold water. We were completely surprised and overwhelmed at their hospitality.

Our guide was Noah, who told us that he was born in 1952. He had a red pickup and on the glove compartment a sticker that said "Hawaii—you be nice to me and I'll be nice to you." We kidded him about that!

Noah took us toward the southern part of the island, once again in the direction of the airport. (Peleliu is only eight miles long and approximately three to four miles wide.)

When LeRoy was there on D-Day, September 15, 1944, there were no trees, no shrubs, nothing on this part of the island, due to the destructive weapon fire of both the Japanese and the Marines. However, in thirty-five years everything had grown, and there were lots of shrubs. Brush and jungle vine had taken over. Even the twelve-thousand-foot runway used during the war, which had been wide, was now reduced to a narrow ribbon through the brush.

Our direction took us toward Bloody Nose Ridge, located to the north and a little east of the airstrip. We could see the monument at the top as we neared the sharp hill. Along the right hand side of the road was an abandoned U.S. alligator, which was still in pretty good condition. Noah informed us that we couldn't drive up to the monument, as the road would soon end.

Monument on top of Bloody Nose Ridge, Peleliu, Palau Islands, erected in 1944.

Nevertheless, determination prevailed; we decided that we would walk the remaining 250 yards to the top. Noah led the way, which was a steady climb through brush and over logs. The last hundred feet were the hardest, as it was straight up. The ferns, leaves, and tree needles made the path very slippery. Noah held my hand and pulled, while LeRoy shoved me from the rear! Soon we were at the top. The engraving on the monument had suffered weather damage, but was still fairly legible. It read, "Lest we forget those who died, 329 Infantry U.S. Army 1944."

From that spot on top we could look down to where LeRoy had been camped during the latter part of his stay on Peleliu. The land was flat and only short grass now covered the spot, which was very wide in area.

We slowly worked our way down the mountainside, back to the pickup, and then drove to where the bivouac area had been. Driving south from there, past the old Japanese ammunition dump, we passed a small harbor where a boat lay on its side. We were told that that particular boat had been used by General MacArthur in the Philippines. When we arrived at the point, we could see White Beach—a beautiful, sandy beach—extending about one and one-half miles long and changing to volcanic rock at the end.

Looking at White Beach, Peleliu where U.S. Forces landed on September 15, 1944. Note old iron drum for ship tie-up still remaining in the ocean waters. Trees and brush have grown along the beach once again.

185

Appendix

A huge iron drum, used for ship tie-ups, was toward the shore not too far from where we were standing looking at White Beach. We used our field glasses in order to find two rocks that LeRoy had hidden between on D-Day, but could not spot them. We assumed, therefore, that more sand had washed ashore since that day, and perhaps the rocks were now hidden by large tall trees and brush.

While he discussed this, along came a native with three children. He had a pickup and some cement bags, which he was planning to fill with sand. We asked him if he knew where the old Marine cemetery had been, and he thought he did. The old Marine cemetery was the spot where the 454th Amphibious Truck Company had camped the second night after the invasion, and was located just alongside of the actual invasion site— right on White Beach. We walked along the road about 600 feet parallel to the beach; then the man started cutting a path through the brush, working his way toward the beach. After about 200 feet we reached two large entry posts beautifully made out of rock and cement, then saw a lot of flat ground—much underbrush but not too many trees. This was the spot we were looking for.

Entrance marker at former Armed Services Cemetery on Peleliu, now completely overgrown. All American bodies were sent back to the U.S. after the war.

We kept asking the man about the two big stones, and he thought he knew where they were. He continued cutting down more brush to make a path. When we arrived at the one big stone which he could remember, it appeared to be the head of the cemetery (about 200 feet from the posts we had already found). It was a large monument built on a pyramid cement base, and very much resembled the monument we had seen on Guadalcanal. There were two etched-out square pieces on two sides of the four-sided cement pillar, in which there could have been plaques at one time. However, there were no plaques now.

With this man, we had found the Marine cemetery of which local natives apparently were not aware, inasmuch as the American bodies had been sent home after the war. Noah said that he would make a sign and place it on the side of the road, and would make a larger pathway into the area for future visitors who may come to view World War II sites.

We walked north on White Beach in search of the two large rocks. LeRoy walked about twenty-five feet in the brush, and Noah and I walked along the edge of the beach. Daylight could be seen through the trees and brush, so we felt that, if the two high-pointed rocks were still there, we would have no trouble in spotting them.

Since we had now reached the volcanic rocks at the north end of the beach, we were convinced that the ones we were looking for were no longer there. LeRoy remembered someone mentioning to him when they were camped below Bloody Nose Ridge that the Marines had pushed the rocks over with a bulldozer.

From here we would go to a picnic area for lunch. We drove toward the north end of the island and passed the old Japanese cement communications building on the left side of the road. About a hundred yards further north was an old pillbox. We also passed two large cement posts further on the road, where there had been a Japanese school at one time. The Japanese were pretty well entrenched on this island up until 1944 and had then left, but there is still a lot of Japanese influence left among the present-day natives. We noticed, also, that most of their names seemed to be of Japanese origin.

The picnic area was very nice—right on the beach. There were two men finishing their lunch, and their road grader was parked along the edge of the road. One of these men confirmed that the Marines had bulldozed the rocks, since there apparently had been a Japanese cave underneath them. This was one way of eliminating those few holdouts!

At that time, since our day had been so successful, and since it was only 2:30 P.M., we decided there was no need for us to stay overnight with Chief Obak. We informed Noah that we would like to take the 4:45 P.M. back to Koror, if we could get on it.

We drove back to town, stopped to visit with Chief Obak to thank him for the lunch and his courtesies, and informed him that we would return to Koror on the late afternoon flight inasmuch as we had our hotel room there. We asked him how much we owed for the lunch, guide, and his trouble. He said that twenty dollars would be sufficient, so we doubled it and gave him forty dollars, which seemed to please him very much. The groceries we had brought from Koror, we told him, were for his family.

Noah informed us he would take us to the airport but advised us that we had plenty of time to visit his office, which was the municipal office of Peleliu—a large green-painted cement building, with a judge's office and a dispensary. It was very clean and neat and was located across the street from the modern school building.

We then proceeded to the airport and visited with some people who came by in a pickup. You see, the airfield was also used as a road. Since there were only two flights a day (a total of four landings since the plane goes to Angaur and returns in a short time each way) there is no reason why vehicles cannot use the runway. Most of the vehicles are pickups made in Japan.

Bob arrived in a short time with his Cessna, landing and unloading his two passengers and his freight. He asked us if we would like to ride the short run to Angaur and back. We jumped at the opportunity. Balang, who had arrived with Reiko to take the plane back to Koror, had gone back with Noah someplace after she saw us at the airfield. Therefore, our pilot assured us he would definitely be stopping at Peleliu, although oftentimes he flies right back from Angaur.

The five-minute flight to Angaur was a spectacular sight. Angaur is located just a little south and west of Peleliu, and the airfield could be spotted almost instantly inasmuch as there is a long cut between the mountain trees. We circled the island from the north, passing right over the village, and then approached the airfield from the west. There was a seven-thousand-foot-long airstrip. Incidentally, Airai (the Babelthuap field where 727s land) is only forty-eight hundred feet long, and we later found out that Yap is four thousand feet long.

The Angaur runway was the nicest of all we had seen. It was black-topped much like a mainland airstrip. They told us it is presently used by the Coast Guard and that during the war it was used by the four-motored B-24s, while the B-26s landed at Peleliu along with corsairs.

When we landed, toward the middle of the field was a shed similar to the one on Peleliu. Two pickups were there and three passengers were waiting to go back to Koror. A big colorful sign read "Angaur International." I quickly hopped off the plane to take a picture of that sign—I couldn't resist!

In just a few minutes we were back in the air on our way to Peleliu. Balang was waiting to be picked up. Lo and behold, she had gone back to town with Noah to pick up a pandanus purse she had made, and gave it to me as a souvenir. I was quite moved by her action and expressed my deep appreciation, which Reiko translated into their native tongue, and gave Balang a kiss on the cheek.

Welcome sign on building at the main dock on Peleliu, Palau Islands.

Appendix

The trip over the Rock Islands going back to Koror was even more spectacular than the morning trip—every island seemed to have its own unique resemblance to an animal or person.

Upon our arrival on Babelthuap, Balang gave us her card and told us to contact her whenever we came to Koror. She and her husband live there but have a home on Peleliu as well.

When we returned to our hotel, the Japanese agent at the tour desk, with whom we had made the arrangements for Peleliu, and who we were seeing in order to pay him the forty dollars for the round-trip flight, informed us that he was taking a boat trip the next day to Peleliu. He asked if we would like to join him. There would only be four of us going and we would take a tour of the Rock Islands on the way back. He assured us that we would enjoy the day. We immediately decided to return to Peleliu!

Our dinner at the hotel that evening consisted of soup or salad with a seafood plate. The seafood consisted of steamed tuna with a cream sauce on top, two deep-fried pieces of taro, a ball of rice, some string beans, and some sashimi in a clam shell (raw fish with coleslaw under it, served with lime and a green Japanese hot sauce). In addition, there was plenty of hot bread, and everything was delicious!

Modern school building in the main part of town, Peleliu, Palau Islands.

Wednesday, April 18 at 9:30 A.M., we were at the hotel dock, loaded into the motorboat. The group included the driver, a young man with two Japanese tourists, and our Japanese tour agent, nicknamed Jo by LeRoy.

The young native sat next to the driver; a cooler containing beer and pop was on the seat behind him. One of the tourists sat next to it, and the second Japanese man, LeRoy, and I were at the back of the boat. Jo merely sat on the flat part of the bow.

The driver started the motor and put it in either the only speed the boat had, or the only speed he knew, which was high—full steam ahead! By the time we had rounded three or four of the Floating Rock Islands, we were commencing to hit rough ocean waters (it had been very calm around the islands). Our driver couldn't see any point in slowing down, as he would be wasting time, so we continued full throttle into the ocean waves.

We bounced through three or four waves, jolting up and down. I made up my mind that I'd rather die in an airplane crash than drown in the ocean, and decided that I'd rather fly home in the air with Bob than fly over the water with this driver!

About that time he hit a wave so hard that it threw us up in the air and the boat came down flat on its bottom. Why we didn't flip completely over is only known by the good Lord. I was sick to my stomach, and only wished that the boat ride would soon end and would not take the customary one hour and twenty minutes to travel from Koror to Peleliu.

LeRoy quickly asked for a life jacket for me. I would have hated to be drowning because it must have taken a good ten minutes to even locate the life jacket, much less try to dislodge it from under the dashboard of the boat. Meanwhile, Jo, perched on the flat deck up front, had been jarred so badly that he had sprained his right ankle. (We later found out from the blood that he had also cut it.)

All of these happenings didn't seem to jar our native driver, but he did head into calmer waters and the balance of our trip was more relaxed in spite of the high speed.

We arrived at the Peleliu dock, which, unlike the airport (located on the southern part of the island), was located on the northern part of the island just about a mile from the town. The sign on the building read, "Welcome to Peleliu."

There was a pickup—several, in fact—waiting at the dock. We quickly gathered the cooler and personal gear aboard it. The driver stayed behind with the boat—apparently there was a gas shortage on Peleliu and one couldn't leave a boat unattended if it had gas in it, for it would be taken and one would be unable to get home.

Our first stop in town was at the school, where Jo wanted the vice principal to follow us in his pickup. We then drove to the local store, which is located near Chief Obak's house. There the Chief was standing, waiting to greet whoever it might be. He was surprised to see us again, but welcomed us warmly. We asked him if he had gotten his bulldozer repaired. He had, but it wasn't working that day, as he had had to send a worker to Koror to get some hydraulic fluid. He took us around to the back of the store and introduced us to his wife, Joanna, and their three-year-old son, who were sitting under a tree.

Several of the town women were preparing a lunch for our group, so the Chief invited us to sit down and eat. He had already had his lunch, but stayed and visited with us.

After lunch the Chief introduced us to a young white couple who were now living on the island. All the property was owned by the natives, but the Chief had permitted this young couple to have one acre on which to live. They had cleared the property and were getting ready to build a home.

About a year earlier they had come to Peleliu, looked the island over, then returned to the States to gather their necessary belongings, including shovels and tools that they would need. They had an eight-year-old son who was attending the local school, which was held in English. They missed their friends and realized that due to the difference in cultures, their friendships on the island were limited. However, they appeared very happy and told us that they were trying to grow tomatoes and vegetables—they were trying to change the diet of the islanders, which consisted primarily of fish, taro, and rice.

During our visit, Jo came back from the hospital where they had bandaged his ankle. He was jumping on his good leg so as not to have to walk on the bad one. Someone gave him a walking stick, so he was in business for the rest of the day!

We were off for the island tour. This was our second trip in two days. Of course it was LeRoy's third one; no doubt he was the only living person who was on Peleliu on D-Day to ever be able to equal that record.

We drove through familiar country—past the old Japanese communication center, the pillbox, and then the airfield. We were on our way to Orange Beach, which was past the boat harbor we had passed the day before. This time, however, we traveled on the side where the MacArthur boat was beached, and then stopped to look over some airplane scraps from the war. We kept saying they were Japanese Zeros, and our two tourist friends kept insisting they were American planes. Imagine two Americans touring an American-Japanese battlefield with four Japanese!

Our tourist friends pawed through the wreckage and found a part that had the metal engraved "Kaiser Corporation, Mfd for Vought Aircraft," or words similar to that, with a serial number stamped thereon. I didn't inspect it too much; about that time I would have liked to find any piece stamped "Nippon," "Japan," or "Hirohito," or any written Japanese language! Every so often they would holler "Corsair" and the old familiar kamikaze smile would erupt.

We remained good friends in spite of it all, but they took home two parts of metal they had salvaged—one was the wing tip of a plane and the other was a large metal apparatus that could have been part of a steering mechanism. I must note here that most of the metal was painted red, and that there were no visible white stars. Only military personnel would be able to identify the types of planes that lay in the scrap pile.

From there we drove to Bloody Nose Ridge and to the end of the road. We did not feel we would undertake the hike up the hill again to the 1944 monument, and our friends did not seem interested enough to try. Along the way we passed the alligator we had seen the day before, but noticed the driver didn't stop. LeRoy did have the driver, who was the vice principal of the local school, drive to the area below the ridge where the 454th had camped so that we could see it once more.

We continued on to Orange Beach and Honeymoon Beach (so named because after the war, according to the natives, this was the place where the officers had their wives come from the United States for rest and relaxation).

Our guide took us to a swimming hole, which was similar to an underground cave and about fifteen feet in diameter. The young Japanese went in for a swim and did a little snorkeling.

From there we drove to a picnic area that is used by the natives, located on a lovely sandy beach. It was Purple Beach, located on the west side of the island. We each had a drink of pop or beer, and then Jo announced it was time to get back to the boat, since it was 3 P.M. However, on the way back we made one last stop—a visit to the Japanese cemetery.

This was really a fun trip, and one we were so glad to have had the opportunity to take, even though we had been there the day before. We saw a few things that we had not seen on Tuesday, and yet we could never have gotten all our work done had we only gone on the boat trip with a group. We decided that our going alone by air, the previous day, had been the smart way to get our work accomplished.

I was dreading the boat ride home, and immediately donned my life jacket. The local Koror-Peleliu mail and freight boat had docked. It was a real old fishing vessel and had just arrived on its daily trip. Natives had arrived at the dock to help unload the freight onto pickups for the trip into the village. Our native driver started the motor on our boat, put it in high, and we were once again off to the races!

Our trip back home, however, was in the calm, interfloating rock island waters, and really a sight to behold. We saw large washouts between rocks, caves, odd-shaped islands, and beautiful views—every turn was a new experience. We stopped along the way for the two natives to snorkel.

At one point our driver dove in, with his snorkeling gear, and returned about five minutes later with one of the huge South Pacific clams. He had already cut the meat out of the immense shell, and was gutting it as he arrived at the boat. He then sliced it into small round steaks, and we ate it with soy sauce and Japanese green mustard. It was luscious!

It was 5:30 P.M. when we returned to our hotel dock, all on extremely friendly terms, telling one another how much we had enjoyed each other's company. Our two Japanese tourists were leaving the next day, so they both wished us lots of luck and a safe journey home.

Koror

No sooner had we arrived in our room than there was a knock at the door. It was Toyoko, the daughter of Balang, with her husband. They had brought us a plastic bag which contained a fresh pineapple, a papaya (black-skinned), and a dozen bananas. We were surprised but very glad to meet them. We offered to have them join us for dinner, but they informed us that Balang needed the car to attend a legislative meeting that night, so they had to get back home.

We then suggested that both of them, with Balang and Techung, join us for dinner on Friday night. Toyoko told us that her mother and father go to Peleliu every Saturday and Sunday, so we suggested that we all meet Sunday night instead.

During the course of our conversation we learned that she had a sister, Rumi, attending college in Walla Walla, Washington, and that Balang wanted to know how long we would be on Koror, as she wanted to give us the address in Walla Walla where we could reach her. (This we have done since our return home, and have had several wonderful meetings with her in our home, together with 454th Army buddy Carl Hodges and his family, who live in Seattle.)

Thursday morning, April 19, we were up early typing from the notes I had made on our two adventuresome visits to Peleliu. Around noon we took our usual taxi and drove to town. We had really enjoyed the oyako domburi we had at the wharf earlier in the week, and we wanted it again. We stopped to pick up enough groceries to hold us for a few days, and returned to our hotel for some serious work.

The next morning we moved our typewriter onto the lanai so we could enjoy the view of the beautiful Floating Rock Islands as we worked. We thought this would be a good time to start revamping the story we had written so far. As we worked we got further and further into the meat of it. Outside of stopping for a 2:30 P.M. snack, we both worked until 9:30 P.M. LeRoy was writing about Peleliu while I worked on our Guadalcanal research. A heavy rainstorm around 4 P.M. caused us to move indoors. We noticed that most of the rain comes from the south, from Peleliu, but after a squall, it clears up and the sky gets blue once again.

Saturday we continued to write until early evening, when Toyoko and her husband brought us two more pineapples, some avocado, and two large bunches of bananas. They dropped by to change our dinner engagement to Monday night, which would be our last night on Koror.

We heard they were having a Sunday night buffet at the hotel for approximately eight dollars, so decided to enjoy it. They served sashimi, taro greens made into a soup, taro roots, green bean salad, humbow, sushi, rolls, two kinds of Jell-O salad, papaya, and watermelon. This was their pre-entrée course. The entrée then consisted of rice, fish, and barbecued beef ribs. I gave up on the entrée, but did return for seconds of the sashimi, sushi, and humbow!

Monday, April 23, we decided to go to downtown Koror to find a carved storyboard as a souvenir of our visit. Our first stop was at a little shop owned and operated by a gentleman who did his own carving. We found a carved turtle with its story on its back, so decided to buy it for twenty-one dollars. From there we drove to the Palau Activity Center, where they had lots of clay pots, pandanus leaf purses, and a few storyboards, all painstakingly made.

When we decided to have lunch, I wanted to take the storyboard we had purchased into the restaurant with us. However, our taxi driver assured us it would be fine to leave it on the car floor—no one would take it. About an hour later, on our return to the car, which was parked directly in front of the eating establishment, the storyboard was gone. We were dumbfounded, and I cursed myself for not having taken it with me. We felt fortunate, nevertheless, that in all our travels, this was the first thing we had lost.

That evening Balang, Techung, and their son, Dr. Singaru Singeo, arrived at our hotel to join us for dinner. Their daughter and her husband had to attend the funeral of some close friend, so were unable to be with us. However, Singaru could speak English and thus became our interpreter. After dinner we went to our hotel room to visit. Balang brought some gifts for me once again—this time a beautiful storyboard, which was a most welcome gift after having lost one earlier in the day, and also a pandanus purse she had made. Techung brought LeRoy a large conch shell which he had found while snorkeling around Peleliu. They gave us not only their daughter's address in Walla Walla, but also their son's address in California, so we could contact them on our return home.

We had so many questions to ask them, and they so very obligingly answered them all. They told us that leaflets had been dropped by the

Americans over Peleliu, and so they knew they were coming. After leaving the island for Babelthuap the Japanese kept them informed of the news, so that they knew what was going on. Since Peleliu was only twenty-five miles south of Koror, they could hear the bombing that was going on. There were approximately fifty thousand Japanese on Babelthuap during the war, and they tried to send reinforcements to Peleliu; one particular time seven boats left with about five hundred men, but they never reached Peleliu—the ships were sunk.

Apparently the Japanese had come to Peleliu long before the war. There was phosphorus on the island, which they were mining, and they employed the natives to work for them. There were approximately ten thousand Japanese forces on Peleliu, and they fought to the bitter end. They knew they would be killed if they evacuated and tried to get to Babelthuap, so they stuck it out. From the news they received, the Japanese knew they could not win the war. One of the great problems was that the reinforcements that were coming to Peleliu did not have the necessary food. The Americans had blockaded the island and their supply ships could not get in. Apparently many died of starvation.

They told us that almost all the homes that were originally there had been destroyed by the terrific bombing and shelling of the island by the Americans. In 1946, some of the Peleliuans returned to Peleliu from Babelthuap. However, on their return they found that the boundary lines of their property were longer evident, and to this day there is still some controversy among the natives over the property lines.

There are only two hundred to two hundred fifty people on Peleliu at this time. Most of the original ones have either moved to Saipan, or are now on Koror or Babelthuap where they can make a living. Apparently the ground on Peleliu is not very good for farming since the war.

Singaru told us that they would like to make some kind of a memorial on Peleliu and also have a museum. LeRoy suggested contacting the VFW or American Legion, asking GIs who were there to send any items they might have and would like to donate. There is so little on Peleliu as of now, that making it into a war memorial would really be a big undertaking. So far, apparently only one other person (a flyer) who was there in the war has returned to visit the island.

We really enjoyed our visit immensely. They invited us to return and told us we could use their home on Peleliu whenever we did.

Appendix

Okinawa

Tuesday, April 24, 1979, we had to leave Koror. The plane from Guam arrived on time, unloaded, then reloaded, and we took off at 11:30 A.M. LeRoy had talked to the captain prior to takeoff, and he told us that after our scheduled stop at Yap, he would make an announcement over the public address system when we were over Ulithi Island (where Mog Mog is located). That is where the 454th had stopped during the war for a beer bust before going to Okinawa.

After a twenty-minute stop at Yap, as promised, the captain pointed out Ulithi Island to the right as we flew toward Guam. Since we were seated on the right side of the plane we had no problem seeing it. To me, it resembled a crocodile with the tail end in the direction we were flying, which was northeast.

We spent the next three days on Guam, renting a car for two days and driving around the island and packing some clothes we were not using to mail home. We had received a large envelope of mail from home, and quickly answered most of it, as we knew we would be busy once we arrived in Okinawa.

Saturday morning, April 28, we were at the airport ready for our two-and-one-half-hour flight to Naha, Okinawa. On our arrival at Naha we had to go through immigration, but we had our necessary visas, so we had no problem. The Okinawa customs went through all our suitcases, including our typewriter case, however.

Naha was a hustle and bustle—all cars being driven on the left side of the street, and there was lots of traffic, bumper to bumper through most of the city. Our hotel was in downtown Kadena (north of Naha) and not far from Okinawa City.

There were lots of Hong Kong–type stores to glance at, and a large arts and crafts market to visit. Since all the natives spoke Ryukyuan, it was apparent that we were going to have a communication problem. Our taxi driver had not been able to communicate with us, but since our hotel manager could speak a little English, we were able to find out that the Kadena Air Force Base was only four blocks away. Outside the hotel we met a chaplain (a major) who was stationed at the base. He suggested we go to the USO in the morning and that they might be able to help us locate the war zones.

Sunday morning at 8:30 A.M. found us talking to the guard on duty at gate number two of Kadena Air Force Base. He seemed very interested in our mission and immediately gave us permission to go on the base. The USO building was only one and a half blocks from the gate, and that was to be our first stop. We asked the young lady at the gift counter if there was a tour bus, inasmuch as we had noticed a sign out by the taxi stand concerning such a thing on Saturdays and Sundays. However, we were told that we had just missed the bus!

While sipping a cup of coffee, pondering our next move, we spotted two young Marines at another table and decided to discuss our problem with them. We bought them each a milkshake and during our conversation they told us that they had the day off. They informed us that they could rent a car right on the base and since they didn't have anything else to do, they would be glad to take us around. We agreed to pay the cost of the car and to buy their meals during the day.

Upper left background on the hillside was the site of the 454th Amphibious Truck Company's campground, located just below Yomitan (also known as Yontan) Airstrip, Okinawa. Note crypts located in the center near the road.

We proceeded to take the Marine base shuttle bus to the rent-a-car office. There we found out that neither one of them had the particular base card necessary to rent a car. However, one of them told us that he had a friend who had one, so he would be glad to get him.

About one-half hour later the three Marines and the two of us were packed into the small compact rental car, ready to head north on the island in the direction of Yomitan.

We had taken a map with us, which we had bought at the hotel and which showed all of Okinawa in English—the only such one we had found. Everything, but everything was written in Ryukyuan. If there weren't Marine and Air Force personnel who spoke English, it would have been impossible to communicate. You'd never know that the Yanks invaded the place and had won the war!

As we drove toward the East China Sea, we passed the town of Namihira. A short distance from there we noticed what seemed to have been an airstrip at one time. However, since it looked deserted, we continued another two miles and arrived at the town of Toya, right on the East China Sea. We stopped at the local fire hall, where lots of equipment

Yomitan (also known as Yontan) Airfield, Okinawa, which is no longer in use. Taken April 29, 1979.

(nine vehicles) and personnel were on duty. We thought they might be able to tell us where Yomitan Airfield used to be, and also the location of a very small island that would be covered with water during high tide.

The young men could speak only their native tongue so I tried a game of charades. We didn't get anywhere but we all did have a good laugh together!

Alone in our endeavors, we continued down the road toward Sobe, which was only a short distance away. On the way there, LeRoy saw some crypts and felt that they looked like the ones he drove past when he was stationed on Okinawa. Nevertheless, we decided to get to Sobe first to see if there was anything familiar there.

We turned down a small street that led to the sea. It was a dead-end; lots of cars were parked at the end and natives were fishing or picnicking on the beach. A coral reef was visible because of the low tide, but it appeared to be too long a strip. LeRoy remembered the small island because one of the DUKWs got hung up there on D-Day.

We checked the coastline further south and also further north, but the island could not be seen. We did notice what could have been a dock at one time to the south. It was apparent from the growth of businesses and homes in the area that the traffic circle could not be located either.

We drove back toward Toya, but stopped along the way to look at the crypts. LeRoy felt sure that those were the crypts—there were two on the left side of a small coral road and one on the right at the foot of the first house.

By then I felt certain that this was the area where he had been camped, inasmuch as I could visualize the Yomitan Airstrip at the top of the hill of this area. I was convinced that when coming from Namihira to Toya we had made a one-half loop in our travels.

We decided to drive back to inspect what had appeared to be an old airstrip. After traveling about two miles we found the strip on the south side of the road on a hillside. We parked the car at the bottom and walked up a side stretch of coral to the top. Sure enough, there was what was once the Yomitan Airfield. It was still very wide at the end we were on, but about a thousand feet westward on the runway was brush, and the strip dwindled down to one lane on either side.

Into the car we went to explore the field. As we crossed the first clump of brush, we spotted many cars. Some fellows had motor-driven airplanes they were diving around the sky, while others were geared up in parachute jumpsuits, acting as though they were soon going to be picked up for a jump. As we drove further down the strip we found a race track set up by two young men who were racing around the rubber-tired bumper track in go-carts. We waited until they got on the right side of the airfield so we could pass.

After about two and one-half miles of runway we came to the end, which was the west side of the island. There was a cross strip there which now is only about three-quarters of a mile long, and which makes a "T" off the main east-west strip. Someone was tearing up the north portion of this latter small strip. There were lots of Japanese signs, but we had no interpreter. I walked north on this part of the strip while LeRoy went south a bit, then headed into the brush going toward the ocean. Pretty soon he whistled so I knew he had found something. He was pretty sure that was the old camp spot and he wanted me to trot along with him.

We went down a small knoll and found a footpath, which we took going toward the west. At the bottom of this small hillside we found a shack with a lone Okinawan living in it. He was in bed, but peeked at us through the open window. He had a small garden for his own use alongside his plywood home. We made gestures showing that we would like to walk further on down if that was OK with him. He shook his head yes.

After we got through the brush, LeRoy saw the two big rocks where his camp had been. We knew we had found the 454th camp area, which was originally at the end of the Yomitan airstrip.

We were convinced that the camp spot was right above the crypts we had seen earlier in Toya. From the camp area, even though there was brush, we could see the buildings in the town which borders the sea. We felt that finding the airstrip and the camp site would be the best we could do because of the growth in the area in thirty-four years. We were happy to have found some significant sights.

After a Kobe steak dinner in Kadena, we decided to see the northernmost part of the island. We drove through Okinawa City, then north via Ishikawa and Yaka Beach, where we walked on the beach and admired the clean white sand and large bay. We continued to Camp Hansen, where we stopped to see if they had any amphibious DUKWs around. They had only alligator-type and buffalo-type amphibious vehicles, so we continued to Nago, and to the part of the island where the Expo had been held in 1975.

There was an armed forces park at Okuma, which the Marines had heard about from their friends, so we decided to visit it even though it was getting dark. We followed the sea for a very long time, and couldn't help but think how lovely it would have been in the daylight.

It was late when we returned to our hotel, but we had been so very thankful to have found these young men who so generously gave of their time to run around the northern part of the island with us.

Monday, April 30, found us back at the Kadena Air Force Base to get an interbase bus to Camp Butler. We had been told there was an Okinawa museum there depicting all the battles in World War II. On arrival at Camp Butler we inquired as to the location of the museum. The young Marine who showed us the direction where it had been also told us that it was closed, but some of the things had been moved to the Japanese War Museum at Naha. We debated as to whether or not we should hire a taxi to take us to Naha. However, we reasoned that the native driver wouldn't be able to communicate with us, so we had best return to Kadena.

On arrival at that base we found out there were several colored shuttle buses. We took a blue one, thinking it would take us to gate number two. However, after riding around the base for about fifty minutes, we ended right back at the bus depot. We finally caught the green shuttle and in about thirty minutes we arrived at our exit gate, frustrated and tired.

On our way back to the hotel we admired some of the beautiful lacquerware that the Okinawans make. Some of these are trays, dishes, jewelry boxes, tables, and chests of drawers—all with a very highly polished gloss. We picked up some postcards to send to LeRoy's Army buddies and decided to call it a day.

We were up early Tuesday morning, typing the last few days' activities. I told LeRoy that in the middle of the night I had gotten the idea that maybe if we went back to Kadena Air Base that we might be able to find a cabdriver there who could speak English. Our problem on Okinawa was that we just were unable to communicate with the people; the ones we had met just didn't speak English. We both thought that the idea was worth trying.

On our way we stopped at the post office to do some of our mailing. Waiting in line in front of me was a gentleman who appeared to be from the United States. To strike up a conversation, I asked him the cost of an airmail postcard to the United States. He informed me that he always sent letters, so he couldn't help me.

However, as we waited in line, LeRoy and the gentleman started conversing. He told us he was retired from the service and that he would be glad to take us around. We told him we wanted to go to Shuri Castle, Suicide Cliff, the Japanese War Museum, and historical sites around Naha. We told him we'd be glad to pay for the gas, plus meals for him and his wife, and that we'd pay him for his time. It was a deal, and an appointment was made to meet him at our hotel at 10 A.M. the next day.

We felt this was our lucky day; we couldn't believe our good fortune! Since it was raining, we walked up the street to find a place where they sold Chinese food. We found a store where they were packing small plastic trays with rice, chicken, fish, a salad, some green peppers, onions, and vegetables. We bought two dishes at three hundred yen each, or approximately $1.50, stopped at a grocery store for some soy sauce and pop, and then went back to the hotel. We were so enthused about finding someone who could speak English and who knew the island. The balance of the day was spent writing the book.

Wednesday, May 2, was a dark, dismal day with heavy rain. Our friend phoned us and suggested we postpone our trip until Thursday, but rain or shine, we would go then, because as he knew, we were leaving Okinawa on Friday. We had really felt the cold on Okinawa. The temperature was in the fifties, and after spending two months in eighty to eightyfive degree temperatures, our thin sweaters weren't protecting us very much. We took advantage of staying indoors to get our packing done and finalize notes. LeRoy wrote some of the book—writing his experiences during the invasion of Okinawa on April 1, 1945.

Thursday morning at 10 A.M. our friends were there to take us on our tour. We drove toward Naha where there was a continuous string of compact cars. We stopped at the shrine for 143 students and 15 teachers who were killed when they would not heed the warning to come out of their cave as the Marines were mopping up the area. A flamethrower was used on the cave and the life-supporting oxygen was snuffed out.

From there we drove to Suicide Cliff, where some Japanese soldiers and civilians had taken their lives. Incense and flowers were sold at the entrance of the memorial and, tour after tour of Japanese and Okinawans were buying them and placing them on the graves.

Our next stop was Nami-no-ue Shrine, next to which is the Buddhist Temple called Gokokuji. Both were destroyed during the war, but have since been rebuilt. The view from Nami-no-ue, which is located high on a hilltop overlooking Naha and the East China Sea, was spectacular. Many young people have their wedding ceremonies there. In fact, one couple had just been married and was leaving as we arrived. Lots of wedding garments are sold in businesses around the area, and there are many photography studios.

We arrived at Shuri Museum at 5:15 P.M. only to find that it closed at 4 P.M. This was a disappointment as we had wanted badly to go through it. Nevertheless, our friends took us to the site of Nakagusuku Castle, which had been built on a high ridge 500 feet above Nakagusuku Bay. During World War II the bay was used as a military harbor; now only a few small fishing vessels could be seen. At the castle site, Okinawan young ladies, in their colorful costumes, posed to take pictures with the many tourists who pay the girls for posing with them.

By then, it was again raining quite hard so we decided to return to Kadena. Our friends insisted they would take us to Naha International Airport in the morning, since they had to go to Naha to the commissary.

Friday, May 4, 1979, was our last day in our research travels. We were ready to head home via Tokyo and Honolulu, where we would spend two weeks with our children, who were arriving from the mainland to meet us.

We felt that we should have stayed on Okinawa a little longer in order to enjoy their arts and crafts, dances, and beautiful costumes, and to visit more of the historical sites, of which there are many. This was the first war zone we had visited on which so much construction, transportation, and people were evident. Okinawa was a great final stop after three months of research.

So came the end of our journey. All that was left to do was to get the facts down on paper and share our current experiences with the many combatants who had once been there. You can be sure that all the servicemen were in our thoughts as we traveled. Our only hope is that our story will bring back many memories of their stays on each island. May only the humorous ones live forever in their memories.

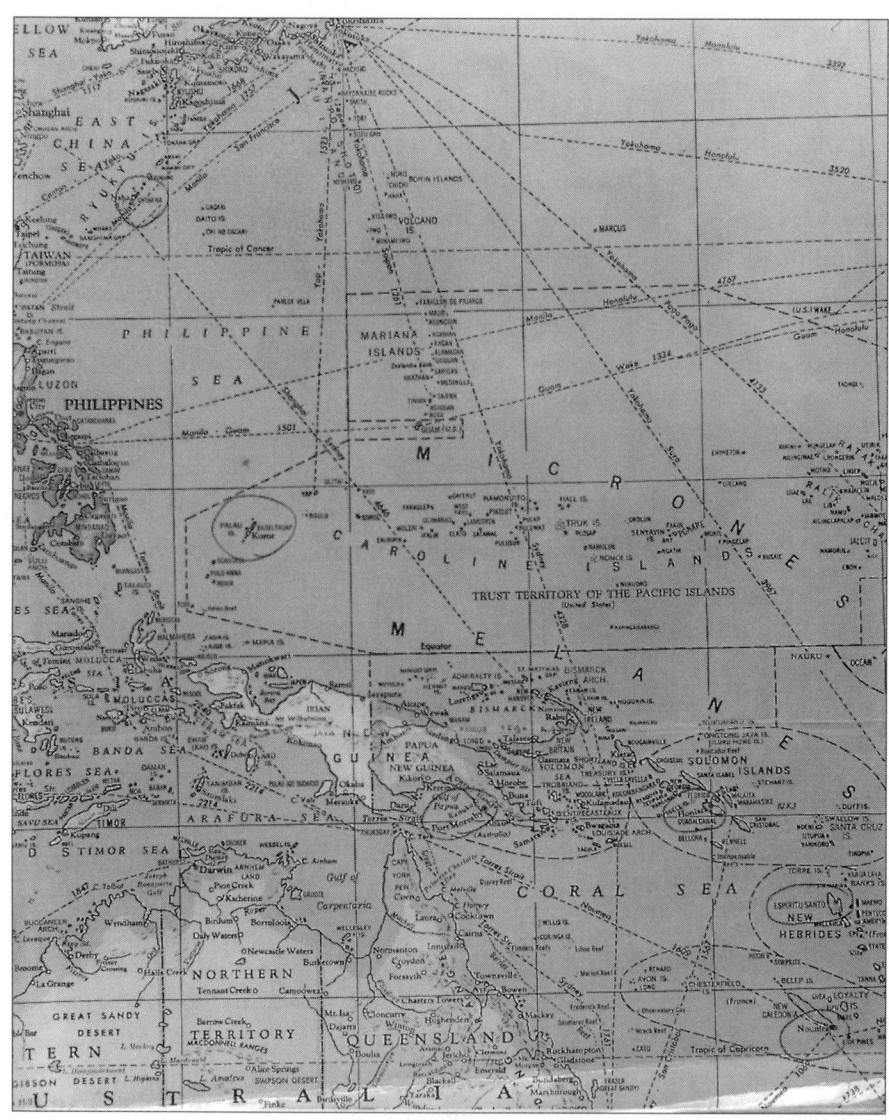

Map of South Pacific Theatre of War

To order additional copies of

Once Upon A Tide

Call (800) 917-BOOK

or send $14.99 each + $3.95 S&H to

Books Etc.
P.O. Box 4888
Seattle, WA 98104